Eyewitness
INVENTION

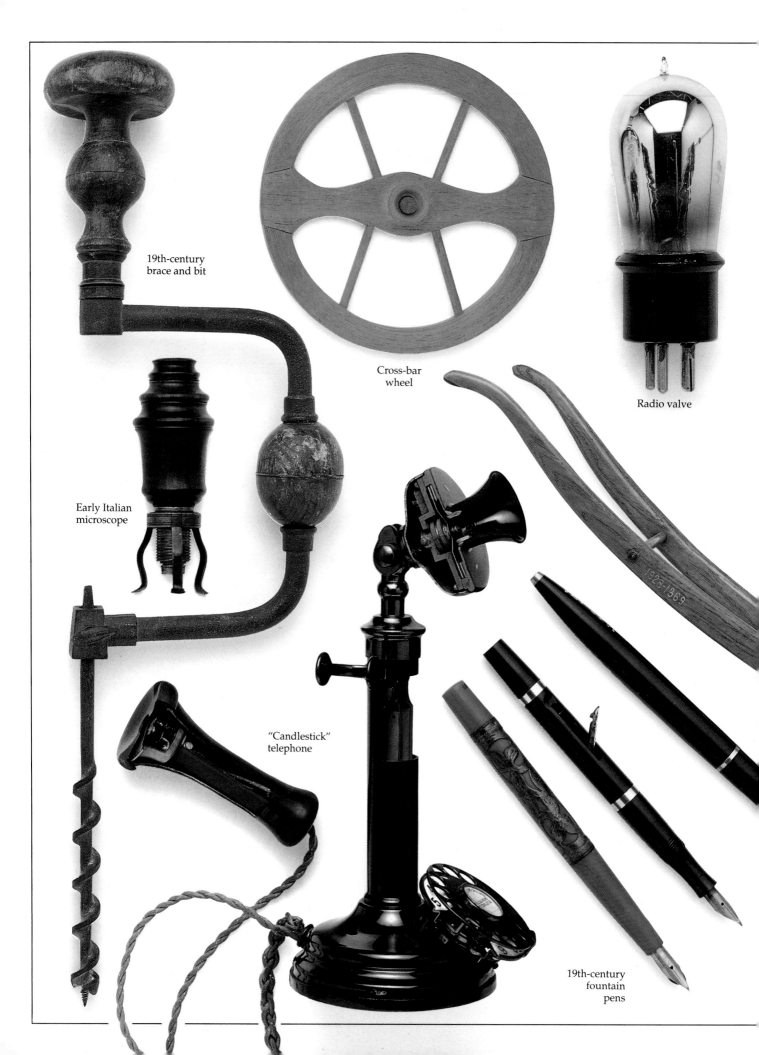

19th-century
brace and bit

Cross-bar
wheel

Radio valve

Early Italian
microscope

"Candlestick"
telephone

1928-1369

19th-century
fountain
pens

Lenses from daguerreotype camera

Ancient Egyptian weights

Eyewitness
INVENTION

Written by
LIONEL BENDER
In association with
THE SCIENCE MUSEUM, LONDON

Roman beam balance

"Napier's bones", 17th-century calculating device

Small's wooden plough

1940s ball point pen

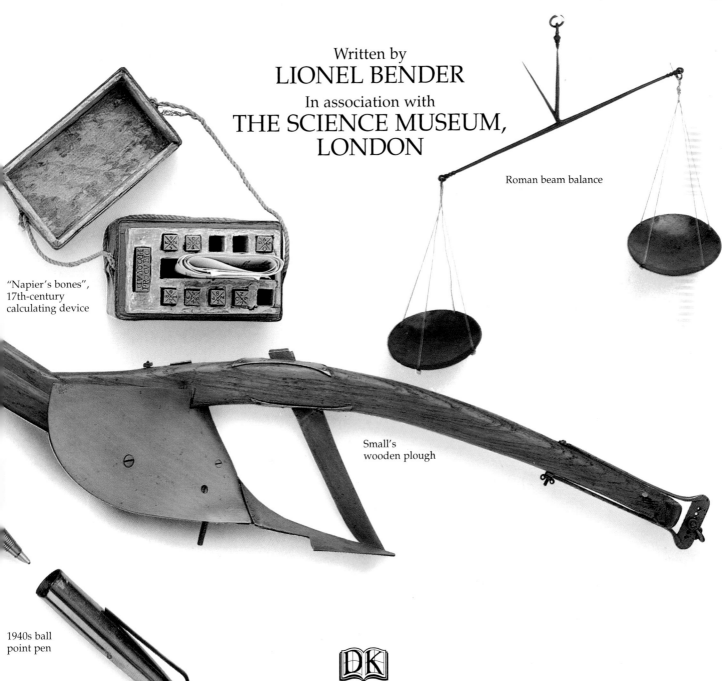

DK

A Dorling Kindersley Book

Chinese measuring calipers

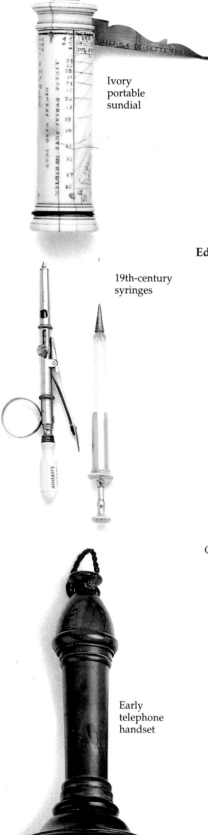

Ivory portable sundial

19th-century syringes

Early telephone handset

Ashanti gold weights

Stone-headed axe from Australia

DK

LONDON, NEW YORK, TORONTO,
MELBOURNE, MUNICH, and DELHI

Project editor Phil Wilkinson
Design Matthewson Bull
Senior editor Helen Parker
Senior art editors Jacquie Gulliver, Julia Harris
Production Louise Barratt
Picture research Kathy Lockley
Special photography Dave King
Additional text Peter Lafferty
Editorial consultants Staff of the Science Museum, London

PAPERBACK EDITION
Managing editors Linda Esposito, Andrew Macintyre
Managing art editor Jane Thomas
Category publisher Linda Martin
Art director Simon Webb
Editor and reference compiler Clare Hibbert
Art editor Joanna Pocock
Consultant Roger Bridgman
Production Jenny Jacoby
Picture research Celia Dearing
DTP designer Siu Yin Ho
2 4 6 8 10 9 7 5 3
This Eyewitness ® Guide has been conceived by
Dorling Kindersley Limited and Editions Gallimard

Hardback edition first published in Great Britain in 1991.
This edition first published in Great Britain in 2003
by Dorling Kindersley Limited,
80 Strand, London WC2R 0RL

A CIP catalogue record for this book is
available from the British Library.

ISBN 0 7513 6489 4

Colour reproduction by
Colourscan, Singapore
Printed in China by Toppan Co. (Shenzhen) Ltd.

See our complete
catalogue at

www.dk.com

Medieval tally sticks

Contents

Chinese mariner's compass

18th-century English compass

What is an invention?

AN INVENTION is something that was devised by human effort and that did not exist before, in contrast to a discovery, which existed but was not yet known. Inventions rarely appear out of the blue. They usually result from the bringing together of existing technologies in a new and unique way. This can happen in response to some specific human need, or as a result of the inventor's desire to do something more quickly or efficiently, or even by accident. An invention can be the result of an individual's work, but is just as likely to come from the work of a team. Inventions can even appear at around the same time in different parts of the world.

Short handle

Pivot

Long blade

Arms allow user to adjust depth and direction of cut

Glass beads

Handle

FOOD FOR THOUGHT
The first tin cans had to be opened by hammer and chisel. In 1855, a British inventor, Yeates, developed this claw type of can opener. The blade cut around the rim of the tin using a see-saw levering action of the handle. Openers were given away with bully beef, hence the bull's head design.

1928-1369

Lid

GLASS
Nobody knows when the process of glass-making (heating together soda and sand) was first discovered, although the Egyptians were making glazed beads in *c.* 2500 B.C. In the 1st century B.C. the Syrians probably introduced glass blowing, producing objects of many different shapes.

CUTTING EDGE
Scissors were invented more than 3,000 years ago, at about the same time in various places. Early types resemble tongs with a spring to push the blades apart. The modern type uses the principle of the pivot and the lever to increase comfort and convenience.

Bull's head

Blade

IN THE CAN
The technique of heating food to a high temperature to kill harmful bacteria then sealing it in airtight containers so that it could be stored for long periods was first perfected by Nicholas Appert in France in 1810. Appert used glass jars sealed with cork, but in 1811 two Englishmen, Donkin and Hall, introduced the use of tin vacuum cans and set up the first food-canning factory.

Lock
mechanism

Iron key

LOCKED UP
In the earliest known locks the key
was used to raise pins or tumblers
so that a bolt could be moved. The
two most common present-day types
are the mortise and the Yale.

ZIP-UP
The zip fastener was invented by
American engineer Whitcomb
Judson in 1893. It consisted of
rows of hooks and eyes which
were locked together by pulling
a slide. The modern version,
with interlocking metal teeth
and slide, was developed from
this by Gideon Sundback and
patented in 1914.

FIRELIGHTERS
Modern matches were
invented by British
chemist John Walker in
1827. He used splinters
of wood tipped with a
mixture of chemicals that
was ignited by heat
generated by the friction
of rubbing the tip on
sandpaper. Matches like
this were later known as
lucifers, from the Latin for
"light bearer".

Bulb from
which air is
extracted

R. BELL'S
IMPROVED
LUCIFERS

Sandpaper

PENCIL-IN THE DETAILS
Pencil "lead" was invented
independently in France and
Austria in the 1790s. Pencil
makers soon discovered that by varying the relative
amounts of the two main components of the lead
(graphite and clay) they could make leads of different
hardnesses.

Winder to take up
tape into container

MASHED UP *below*
Paper was first produced in China around
50 B.C. The earliest examples were made from
a mixture of cloth, wood, and straw (p. 19).

LIGHTING-UP TIME *left*
The electric light bulb evolved from
early experiments which showed
that an electric current flowing
through a wire creates heat due to
resistance in the wire. If the current
is strong enough, the wire glows
white-hot. There were several
independent inventors, including
Thomas Edison and Joseph Swan.
Carbon-filament lamps were mass-
produced from the early 1880s.

Circuit
connector

Paper scroll

**GETTING THE
MEASURE OF IT** *above*
The tape measure evolved from the measuring chains
and rods first used by the Egyptians and then the
Greeks and Romans. This example
incorporates a notebook and
dates from 1846.

Linen tape

Coulter to
cut loose the
soil

Harness link to
attach team of horses
or oxen

IN THE SOIL
The plough developed in about
5000 B.C. from simple hoes and digging
sticks that had been used by farmers for
thousands of years. By changing the
shape and size of its various parts
it was gradually found that
the soil could be cut,
loosened, and turned
in one operation.

Share to cut loose
top layer of soil

Mouldboard to
lift and turn soil

The story of an invention

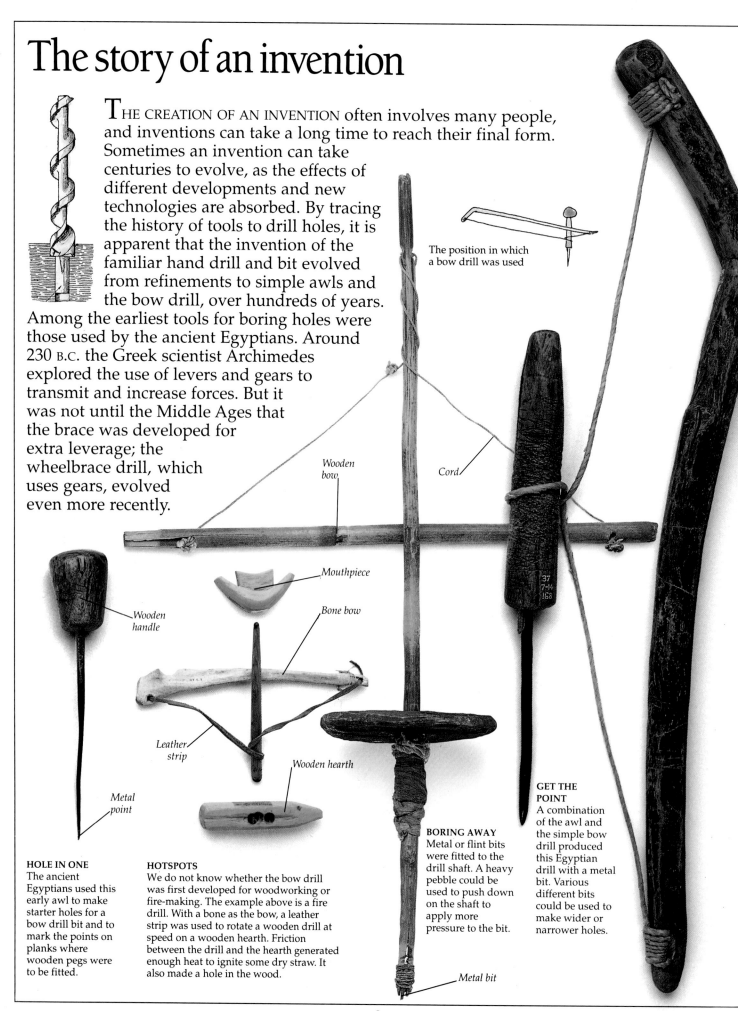

THE CREATION OF AN INVENTION often involves many people, and inventions can take a long time to reach their final form. Sometimes an invention can take centuries to evolve, as the effects of different developments and new technologies are absorbed. By tracing the history of tools to drill holes, it is apparent that the invention of the familiar hand drill and bit evolved from refinements to simple awls and the bow drill, over hundreds of years. Among the earliest tools for boring holes were those used by the ancient Egyptians. Around 230 B.C. the Greek scientist Archimedes explored the use of levers and gears to transmit and increase forces. But it was not until the Middle Ages that the brace was developed for extra leverage; the wheelbrace drill, which uses gears, evolved even more recently.

The position in which a bow drill was used

Wooden bow

Cord

Mouthpiece

Bone bow

Wooden handle

Leather strip

Wooden hearth

Metal point

HOLE IN ONE
The ancient Egyptians used this early awl to make starter holes for a bow drill bit and to mark the points on planks where wooden pegs were to be fitted.

HOTSPOTS
We do not know whether the bow drill was first developed for woodworking or fire-making. The example above is a fire drill. With a bone as the bow, a leather strip was used to rotate a wooden drill at speed on a wooden hearth. Friction between the drill and the hearth generated enough heat to ignite some dry straw. It also made a hole in the wood.

BORING AWAY
Metal or flint bits were fitted to the drill shaft. A heavy pebble could be used to push down on the shaft to apply more pressure to the bit.

37
7-14
168

GET THE POINT
A combination of the awl and the simple bow drill produced this Egyptian drill with a metal bit. Various different bits could be used to make wider or narrower holes.

Metal bit

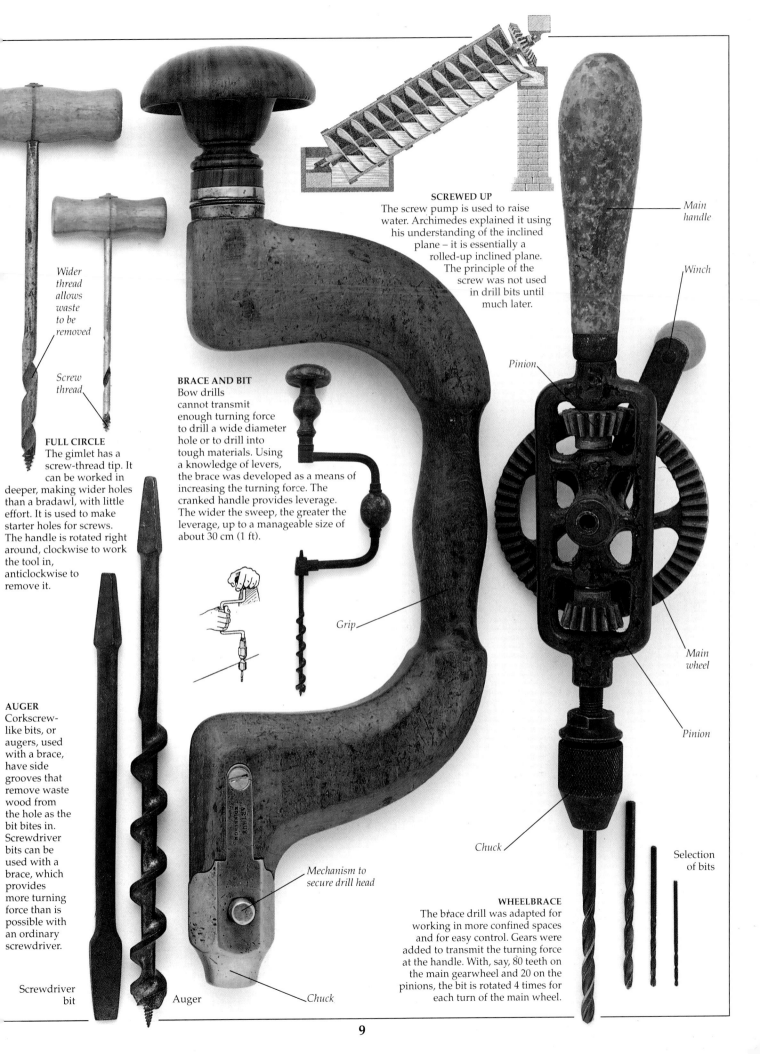

Wider thread allows waste to be removed

Screw thread

FULL CIRCLE
The gimlet has a screw-thread tip. It can be worked in deeper, making wider holes than a bradawl, with little effort. It is used to make starter holes for screws. The handle is rotated right around, clockwise to work the tool in, anticlockwise to remove it.

SCREWED UP
The screw pump is used to raise water. Archimedes explained it using his understanding of the inclined plane – it is essentially a rolled-up inclined plane. The principle of the screw was not used in drill bits until much later.

BRACE AND BIT
Bow drills cannot transmit enough turning force to drill a wide diameter hole or to drill into tough materials. Using a knowledge of levers, the brace was developed as a means of increasing the turning force. The cranked handle provides leverage. The wider the sweep, the greater the leverage, up to a manageable size of about 30 cm (1 ft).

Grip

Main handle

Winch

Pinion

Main wheel

Pinion

AUGER
Corkscrew-like bits, or augers, used with a brace, have side grooves that remove waste wood from the hole as the bit bites in. Screwdriver bits can be used with a brace, which provides more turning force than is possible with an ordinary screwdriver.

Screwdriver bit

Auger

Mechanism to secure drill head

Chuck

Chuck

Selection of bits

WHEELBRACE
The brace drill was adapted for working in more confined spaces and for easy control. Gears were added to transmit the turning force at the handle. With, say, 80 teeth on the main gearwheel and 20 on the pinions, the bit is rotated 4 times for each turn of the main wheel.

Tools

ABOUT 3.75 MILLION YEARS AGO our distant ancestors evolved an upright stance, and began to live on open grassland. With their hands free for new uses, they scavenged abandoned carcasses and gathered plant food. Gradually, early people developed the use of tools. They used pebbles and stones to cut meat and to smash open bones for marrow. Later they chipped away at the edges of their stones, so that they could cut better. Nearly two million years ago, flint was being shaped into axes and arrow-heads, and bones were used as clubs and hammers. About 1.4 million years ago, humankind discovered fire. Now able to cook food, our recent ancestors created a varied toolkit for hunting wild animals. When they started to farm, a different set of tools was needed.

DUAL-PURPOSE IMPLEMENT
The adze was a development of the axe that appeared in the 8th millenium B.C. Its blade was set almost at right-angles to the handle. This North Papuan tool could be used either as an axe (as here) or an adze, by changing the position of the blade.

Stone blade

Split wooden handle

STICKY END
This axe from Australia represents the first stage on from the hand axe. A stone was set in gum in the bend of a flexible strip of wood, and the two halves of the piece of wood were bound together. The axe was probably used to kill wild animals.

GETTING STONED
This flint handaxe, found in Kent, England, was probably worked first with a stone hammer (above), to get the rough shape, then with a bone one. It is perhaps 20,000 years old. It dates from a period known as the Old Stone Age, or Paleolithic period, when flint was the main material for tools.

Socket to take shaft

Hole for binding cord

NEXT BEST THING
Where flint was not available, softer stones were used for tools, as with this rough-stone axe-head. Not all stones could be made as sharp as flint.

AXE TO GRIND
To make this axe-head, a lump of stone was probably rubbed against rocks and ground with pebbles until it was smooth and polished.

WELL-BRONZED
The use of bronze for tools and weapons began in Asia about 8,000 years ago; in Europe the Bronze Age lasted from about 2000 to 500 B.C.

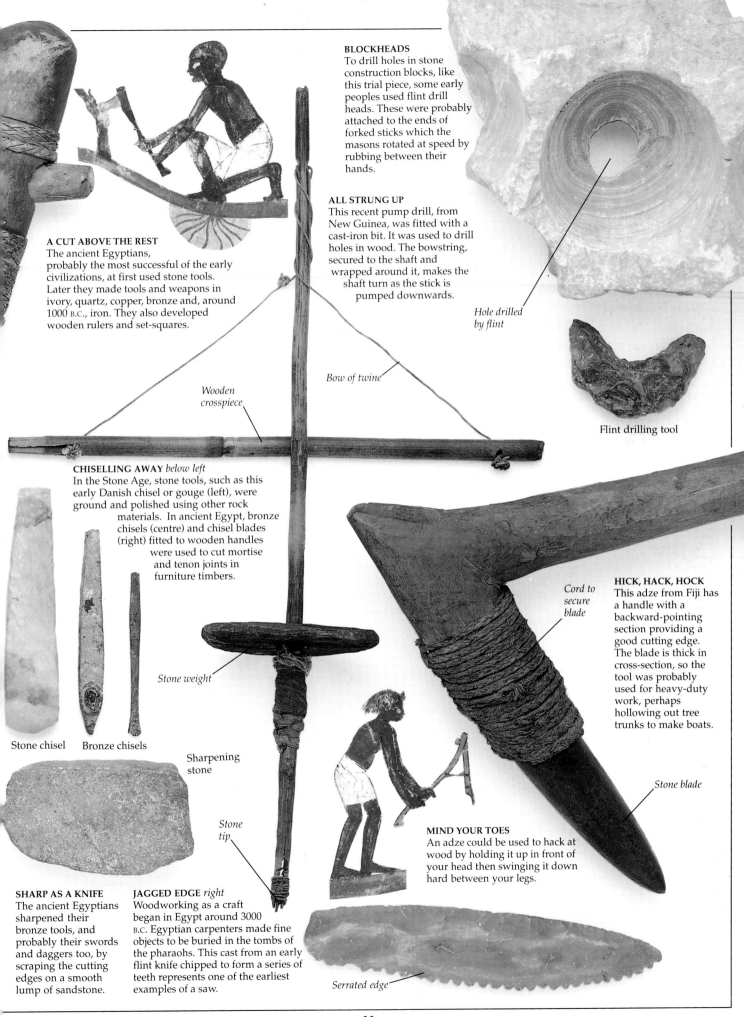

BLOCKHEADS
To drill holes in stone construction blocks, like this trial piece, some early peoples used flint drill heads. These were probably attached to the ends of forked sticks which the masons rotated at speed by rubbing between their hands.

A CUT ABOVE THE REST
The ancient Egyptians, probably the most successful of the early civilizations, at first used stone tools. Later they made tools and weapons in ivory, quartz, copper, bronze and, around 1000 B.C., iron. They also developed wooden rulers and set-squares.

ALL STRUNG UP
This recent pump drill, from New Guinea, was fitted with a cast-iron bit. It was used to drill holes in wood. The bowstring, secured to the shaft and wrapped around it, makes the shaft turn as the stick is pumped downwards.

Hole drilled by flint

Bow of twine

Wooden crosspiece

Flint drilling tool

CHISELLING AWAY *below left*
In the Stone Age, stone tools, such as this early Danish chisel or gouge (left), were ground and polished using other rock materials. In ancient Egypt, bronze chisels (centre) and chisel blades (right) fitted to wooden handles were used to cut mortise and tenon joints in furniture timbers.

Stone weight

Stone chisel   Bronze chisels

Sharpening stone

Cord to secure blade

HICK, HACK, HOCK
This adze from Fiji has a handle with a backward-pointing section providing a good cutting edge. The blade is thick in cross-section, so the tool was probably used for heavy-duty work, perhaps hollowing out tree trunks to make boats.

Stone blade

Stone tip

MIND YOUR TOES
An adze could be used to hack at wood by holding it up in front of your head then swinging it down hard between your legs.

SHARP AS A KNIFE
The ancient Egyptians sharpened their bronze tools, and probably their swords and daggers too, by scraping the cutting edges on a smooth lump of sandstone.

JAGGED EDGE *right*
Woodworking as a craft began in Egypt around 3000 B.C. Egyptian carpenters made fine objects to be buried in the tombs of the pharaohs. This cast from an early flint knife chipped to form a series of teeth represents one of the earliest examples of a saw.

Serrated edge

The wheel

THE WHEEL is probably the most important mechanical invention of all time. Wheels are found in most machines, in clocks, windmills, and steam engines, as well as in vehicles such as the automobile and the bicycle. The wheel first appeared in Mesopotamia, part of modern Iraq, over 5,000 years ago. It was used by potters to help work their clay, and at around the same time wheels were fitted to carts, transforming transport and making it possible to move heavy materials and bulky objects with relative ease. These early wheels were solid, cut from sections of wooden planks which were fastened together. Spoked wheels appeared later, from around 2000 B.C. They were lighter, and were used for chariots. Bearings, which enabled the wheel to turn more easily, appeared around 100 B.C.

POTTER'S WHEEL
By 300 B.C. the Greeks and Egyptians had invented the kick-wheel. The disc's weight meant that it turned at constant speed.

Tripartite wheel

Protective shield for driver

Fixed wooden axle

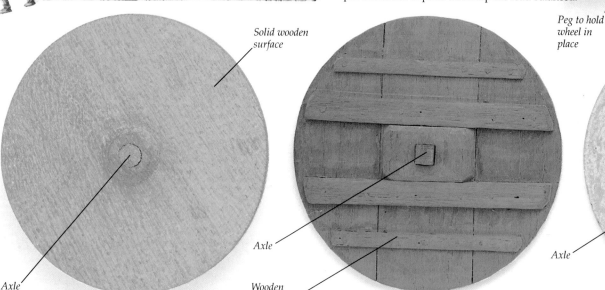

STONE-AGE BUILDERS *left*
Before the wheel, rollers made from tree trunks were probably used to push objects such as huge building stones into place. The tree trunks had the same effect as wheels, but a lot of effort was needed to put the rollers in place and keep the load balanced.

Peg to hold wheel in place

Solid wooden surface

Axle

Axle

Wooden cross-piece

Axle

SCARCE BUT SOLID
Early wheels were sometimes solid discs of wood cut from tree trunks. These were not common as the wheel originated in places where trees were scarce. Solid wooden chariot wheels have been found in Denmark.

PLANK WHEEL
Three-part (or "tripartite") wheels were made of planks fastened together by wooden or metal cross-pieces. One of the earliest forms of wheel, they are still used in some countries. They are suitable for bad roads.

ROLLING STONE
In some places, where wood was scarce, stone was used for wheels instead. It was heavy, but long-lasting. The stone wheel originated in China and Turkey.

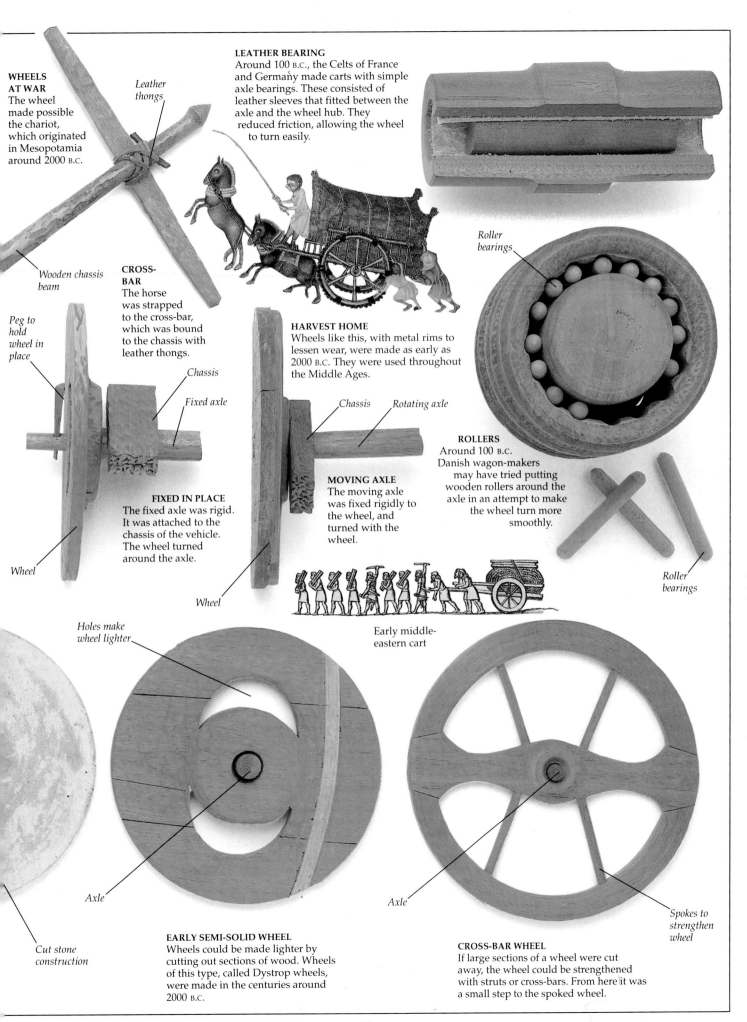

WHEELS AT WAR
The wheel made possible the chariot, which originated in Mesopotamia around 2000 B.C.

Leather thongs

LEATHER BEARING
Around 100 B.C., the Celts of France and Germany made carts with simple axle bearings. These consisted of leather sleeves that fitted between the axle and the wheel hub. They reduced friction, allowing the wheel to turn easily.

Wooden chassis beam

CROSS-BAR
The horse was strapped to the cross-bar, which was bound to the chassis with leather thongs.

Peg to hold wheel in place

Chassis

Fixed axle

Roller bearings

HARVEST HOME
Wheels like this, with metal rims to lessen wear, were made as early as 2000 B.C. They were used throughout the Middle Ages.

Chassis

Rotating axle

FIXED IN PLACE
The fixed axle was rigid. It was attached to the chassis of the vehicle. The wheel turned around the axle.

Wheel

MOVING AXLE
The moving axle was fixed rigidly to the wheel, and turned with the wheel.

ROLLERS
Around 100 B.C. Danish wagon-makers may have tried putting wooden rollers around the axle in an attempt to make the wheel turn more smoothly.

Wheel

Roller bearings

Early middle-eastern cart

Holes make wheel lighter

Cut stone construction

Axle

Axle

Spokes to strengthen wheel

EARLY SEMI-SOLID WHEEL
Wheels could be made lighter by cutting out sections of wood. Wheels of this type, called Dystrop wheels, were made in the centuries around 2000 B.C.

CROSS-BAR WHEEL
If large sections of a wheel were cut away, the wheel could be strengthened with struts or cross-bars. From here it was a small step to the spoked wheel.

Metalworking

GOLD AND SILVER occur naturally in their metallic state. From early times, people found lumps of these metals and used them for simple ornaments. But the first useful metal to be worked was copper, which had to be extracted from rocks, or ores, by heating on a fierce fire. The next step was to make bronze. This is an alloy, made by mixing two metals together. Bronze, an alloy of copper and tin, was strong and did not rust or decay. It was easy to work by melting and pouring into a shaped mould, a process called casting. Because bronze was strong as well as being easy to work, everything from swords to jewellery was made of the metal. Iron was first used around 2000 B.C. Iron ores were burnt with charcoal, producing an impure form of the metal. Iron was plentiful, but difficult to melt; at first it had to be worked by hammering rather than casting.

Roman iron nail, about 88 A.D.

CASTING – FINAL STAGE
When cold, the mould was broken open and the object removed. Solid bronze is far harder than copper, and can be hammered to give a sharp cutting edge. Because of this, bronze became the first metal to be widely used.

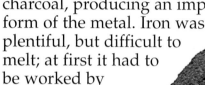

Bloom of iron

Iron ore

Partially hammered bloom

BLOOM OF IRON
Early furnaces were not hot enough to melt iron and so the metal was produced as a spongy lump, called a bloom. The bloom was hammered into shape while red hot.

CASTING – FIRST STAGE
The first stage in producing bronze was to heat copper and tin ores in a large bowl or a simple furnace. Bronze is easier to melt and separate than copper alone.

CASTING – SECOND STAGE
The molten bronze was poured into a mould and allowed to cool and solidify. This process is called casting. Knowledge of bronze casting had reached Europe by about 3500 B.C. and China several centuries later.

IRON SWORD-MAKING
In the first century A.D., iron swords were made by twisting and hammering together several strips or rods of iron. This process was called pattern welding.

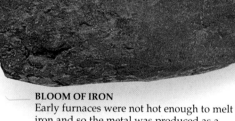

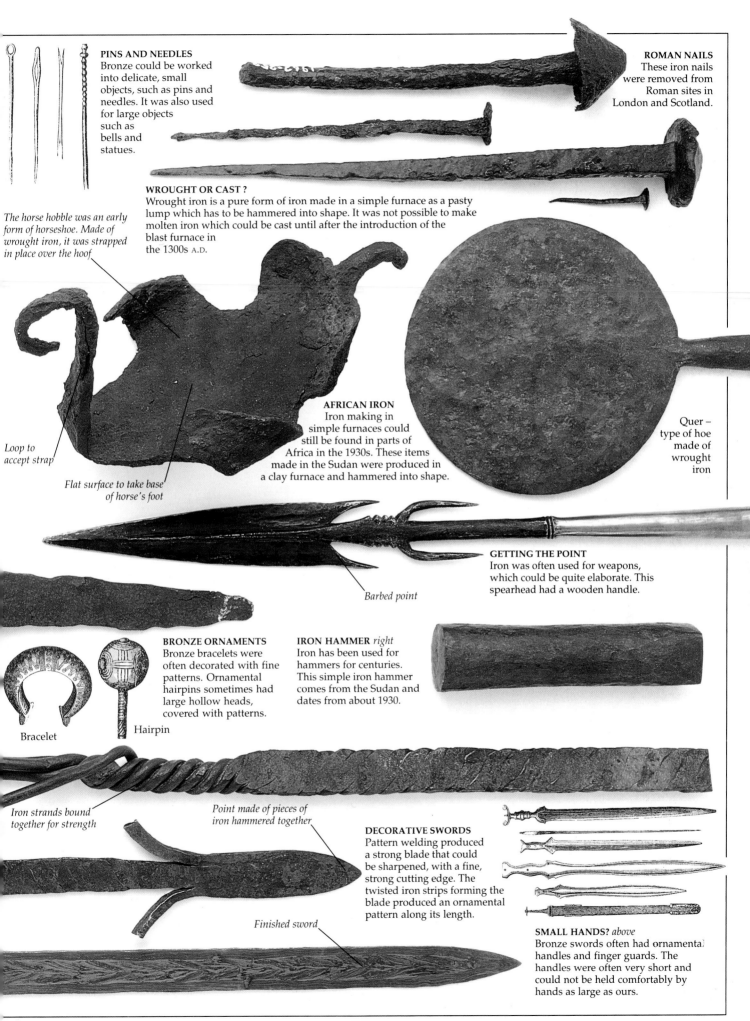

PINS AND NEEDLES
Bronze could be worked into delicate, small objects, such as pins and needles. It was also used for large objects such as bells and statues.

ROMAN NAILS
These iron nails were removed from Roman sites in London and Scotland.

The horse hobble was an early form of horseshoe. Made of wrought iron, it was strapped in place over the hoof

WROUGHT OR CAST ?
Wrought iron is a pure form of iron made in a simple furnace as a pasty lump which has to be hammered into shape. It was not possible to make molten iron which could be cast until after the introduction of the blast furnace in the 1300s A.D.

Loop to accept strap

AFRICAN IRON
Iron making in simple furnaces could still be found in parts of Africa in the 1930s. These items made in the Sudan were produced in a clay furnace and hammered into shape.

Flat surface to take base of horse's foot

Quer – type of hoe made of wrought iron

Barbed point

GETTING THE POINT
Iron was often used for weapons, which could be quite elaborate. This spearhead had a wooden handle.

BRONZE ORNAMENTS
Bronze bracelets were often decorated with fine patterns. Ornamental hairpins sometimes had large hollow heads, covered with patterns.

Bracelet

Hairpin

IRON HAMMER *right*
Iron has been used for hammers for centuries. This simple iron hammer comes from the Sudan and dates from about 1930.

Iron strands bound together for strength

Point made of pieces of iron hammered together

DECORATIVE SWORDS
Pattern welding produced a strong blade that could be sharpened, with a fine, strong cutting edge. The twisted iron strips forming the blade produced an ornamental pattern along its length.

Finished sword

SMALL HANDS? *above*
Bronze swords often had ornamental handles and finger guards. The handles were often very short and could not be held comfortably by hands as large as ours.

Weights and measures

THE FIRST SYSTEMS of weights and measures were developed in ancient Egypt and Babylon. They were needed to weigh crops, measure plots of farmland, and to standardize commercial transactions. Around 3500 B.C. the Egyptians were using scales; they had standard weights and a measurement of length called the cubit equal to about 52 cm (21 in). The Code of Hammurabi, a document recording the laws of the king of Babylon from 1792 to 1750 B.C., refers to standard weights and different units of weight and length. By Greek and Roman times, scales, balances, and rulers were in everyday use. Present-day systems of weights and measures, the imperial (foot, pound) and metric (metre, gram), were established in the 1300s and 1790s respectively.

Early Egyptian stone weights

Metal Egyptian weights

Hook for object to be weighed

HEAVY METAL
Early Egyptians used rocks as standard weights but around 2000 B.C., as metal-working developed, weights cast in bronze and iron were used.

WORTH THEIR WEIGHT IN GOLD
The Ashanti, Africans from a gold-mining region of modern Ghana, rose to power in the 18th century. They made standard weights in the form of gold ornaments.

Fish

Sword

Scorpion

WEIGHING HIM UP
This ancient Egyptian balance is being used in a ceremony called "Weighing the heart", which was supposed to take place after a person's death.

Pointer

OFF BALANCE
This Roman beam balance for weighing coins consists of a bronze rod pivoted at the centre. Objects to be weighed were placed on a pan hung from one end of the beam and were balanced against known weights hung from the other end. A pointer at the centre of the beam showed when the pans balanced.

Pan

Hollow to take smaller weights

WEIGHTY NEST EGGS
With simple balances, sets of standard weights are used. You put on or take off large or small weights until the balance is horizontal. These are French 17th-century nesting weights, one fitting neatly into another to make a neat stack.

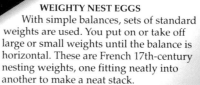

Scale in inches and centimetres

USING THE STEELYARD *right*
On a steelyard, the weight is moved along the long arm and the distance from the pivot to the balance-point, read off the scale, gives the object's weight. For travelling merchants, its advantage was that you did not have to carry a large range of weights.

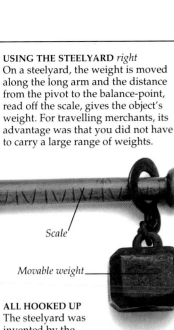

Scale

Movable weight

STICKING TO ONE'S PRINCIPLES
The first official standard yard was established by King Edward I of England in 1305. It was an iron bar divided into 3 feet of 12 inches each. This is a 19th-century tailor's yardstick used to measure lengths of cloth. It also has a centimetre scale.

Foot positioned here

Adjustable jaw

ALL HOOKED UP
The steelyard was invented by the Romans around 200 B.C. Unlike a simple balance it had one arm longer than the other. A sack of grain, say, would be hung from the short arm and a single weight moved along the long arm, until it balanced. This example dates from the 17th century.

GRIPPED TIGHT *above right*
Spanner-like sliding calipers, used to measure the width of solid objects such as stone, metal, and wooden building components, were invented at least 2,000 years ago. Measurements are read off a scale on a fixed arm as on this replica of a caliper from China.

A BIG STEP *above right*
This British size stick for measuring people's feet starts with size 1 as a 4.33 inch length and increases by stages of one-third of an inch.

FLEXIBLE FRIEND *left*
Tape measures are used in situations where a ruler is too rigid. Measuring people for clothes is one of the most familiar uses of the tape measure, but much longer tapes are also used.

FILLED TO THE BRIM *below*
Liquids must be placed in a container, such as this copper jug used by a distiller, in order to be measured. The volume mark is in the narrow part of the neck, so the right measure can instantly be seen.

GETTING IT RIGHT
One of the most important things about weights and measures is that they should be standardized, so that each unit is always identical. These men are testing weights and liquid measures to ensure they are accurate.

Volume mark here

NO SHORT MEASURES
This Indian grain measure was used to dispense standard quantities of loose items. A shopkeeper would sell the grain by the measureful rather than weigh up different quantities each time.

Pen and ink

WRITTEN RECORDS first became necessary with the development of agriculture in the Fertile Crescent in the Middle East about 7,000 years ago. The Babylonians and ancient Egyptians inscribed stones, bones, and clay tablets with symbols and simple pictures. They used these records to establish land tenure and irrigation rights, to keep records of harvests, and write down tax assessments and accounts. As writing implements they first used flints, then the whittled ends of sticks. Around 2500 B.C. the Chinese and Egyptians developed inks made from lampblack, obtained from the oil burnt in lamps, mixed with water and plant gums. They could make different coloured inks from earth pigments such as red ochre. Oil-based inks were developed in the Middle Ages for use in printing (p. 26–27), but writing inks, and lead pencils are quite modern inventions. More recent developments, such as the fountain pen and the ball-point, were designed to get the ink on the paper without the need to keep refilling the pen.

LIGHT AS A FEATHER
A quill – the hollow shaft of a feather – was first used as a pen around A.D. 500. Dried and cleaned goose, swan, or turkey feathers were most popular because the thick shaft held the ink and the pen was easy to handle. The tip was shaved to a point with a knife and split slightly to ensure that the ink flowed smoothly.

HEAVY READING
The first writing that we have evidence of is on Mesopotamian clay tablets. Scribes used a wedge-shaped stylus to make marks in the clay while it was wet. The clay set to leave a permanent record. The marks that make up this sort of writing are called cuneiform, meaning wedge-shaped.

A PRESSING POINT
In the 1st millenium B.C. the Egyptians wrote with reeds and rushes, which they cut to form a point. They used the reed pens to apply lampblack to papyrus.

余枚戋

Chinese characters

ON PAPYRUS
Ancient Egyptian and Assyrian scribes wrote on papyrus. This was made from pith taken from the stem of the papyrus plant. The pith was removed, arranged in layers, and hammered to make a sheet. The scribe (left) is recording a battle. The papyrus (right) is from ancient Egypt.

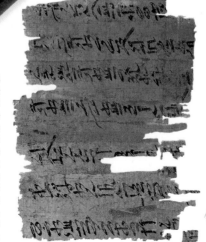

STROKE OF GENIUS
The ancient Chinese wrote their characters in ink using brushes of camels' or rats' hairs. Clusters of hairs were glued and bound to the end of a stick. For fine work on silk they used brushes made of just a few hairs glued into the end of a hollow reed. All 10,090 or more Chinese characters are based on just eight basic brushstrokes.

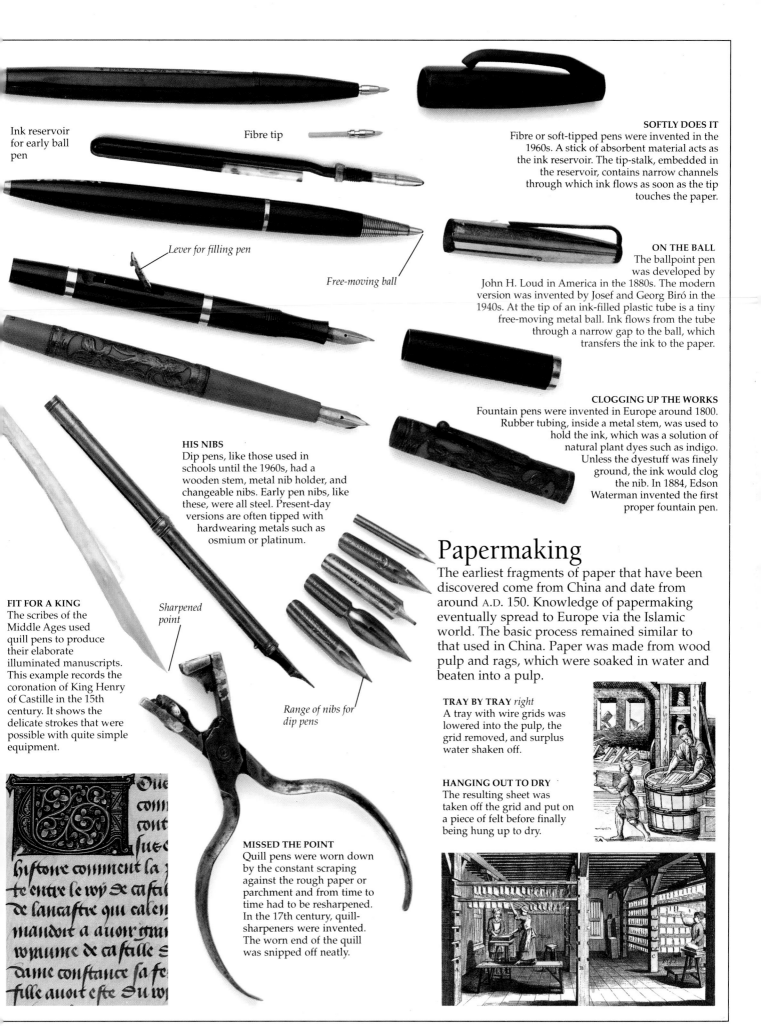

Ink reservoir for early ball pen

Fibre tip

Lever for filling pen

Free-moving ball

SOFTLY DOES IT
Fibre or soft-tipped pens were invented in the 1960s. A stick of absorbent material acts as the ink reservoir. The tip-stalk, embedded in the reservoir, contains narrow channels through which ink flows as soon as the tip touches the paper.

ON THE BALL
The ballpoint pen was developed by John H. Loud in America in the 1880s. The modern version was invented by Josef and Georg Biró in the 1940s. At the tip of an ink-filled plastic tube is a tiny free-moving metal ball. Ink flows from the tube through a narrow gap to the ball, which transfers the ink to the paper.

CLOGGING UP THE WORKS
Fountain pens were invented in Europe around 1800. Rubber tubing, inside a metal stem, was used to hold the ink, which was a solution of natural plant dyes such as indigo. Unless the dyestuff was finely ground, the ink would clog the nib. In 1884, Edson Waterman invented the first proper fountain pen.

HIS NIBS
Dip pens, like those used in schools until the 1960s, had a wooden stem, metal nib holder, and changeable nibs. Early pen nibs, like these, were all steel. Present-day versions are often tipped with hardwearing metals such as osmium or platinum.

Papermaking
The earliest fragments of paper that have been discovered come from China and date from around A.D. 150. Knowledge of papermaking eventually spread to Europe via the Islamic world. The basic process remained similar to that used in China. Paper was made from wood pulp and rags, which were soaked in water and beaten into a pulp.

FIT FOR A KING
The scribes of the Middle Ages used quill pens to produce their elaborate illuminated manuscripts. This example records the coronation of King Henry of Castille in the 15th century. It shows the delicate strokes that were possible with quite simple equipment.

Sharpened point

Range of nibs for dip pens

TRAY BY TRAY *right*
A tray with wire grids was lowered into the pulp, the grid removed, and surplus water shaken off.

HANGING OUT TO DRY
The resulting sheet was taken off the grid and put on a piece of felt before finally being hung up to dry.

MISSED THE POINT
Quill pens were worn down by the constant scraping against the rough paper or parchment and from time to time had to be resharpened. In the 17th century, quill-sharpeners were invented. The worn end of the quill was snipped off neatly.

Lighting

THE FIRST ARTIFICIAL LIGHT came from fire, but this was dangerous and difficult to carry around. Then, some 20,000 years ago, people realized that they could get light by burning oil, and the first lamps appeared. These were hollowed-out rocks full of animal fat. Lamps with wicks of vegetable fibres were first made in about 1000 B.C. At first, they had a simple channel to hold the wick; later, the wick was held in a spout. Candles appeared about 5,000 years ago. A candle is just a wick surrounded by wax or tallow. When the wick is lit, the flame melts some of the wax or tallow, which burns to give off light. So a candle is really an oil lamp in a more convenient form. Oil lamps and candles were the chief source of artificial light until gas lighting became common in the 19th century; electric lighting took over more recently.

CAVE LIGHT
When early people made fire for cooking and heating, they realised that it also gave off light. So the cooking fire provided the first source of artificial light. From this it was a simple step to make a brushwood torch, so that light could be carried, or placed high up in a dark cave.

SHELL-SHAPED *right*
By putting oil in the body and laying a wick in the neck, a shell could be used as a lamp. This one was used in the 19th century, but shell lamps were made centuries before.

Wick

COSTLY CANDLES
The first candles were made over 5,000 years ago. Wax or tallow was poured over a hanging wick and left to cool. Such candles were too expensive for most people.

Container for wax

Wick

Spout for wick

UP THE SPOUT
Saucer-like pottery lamps have been made for thousands of years. They burned olive oil or oil from colza, the root of the swede. This one was probably made in Egypt, about 2,000 years ago.

COVERED OVER *right*
The Romans made clay lamps with a covered top to keep the oil clean. They sometimes had more than one spout and wick, to give a stronger light.

Hole for wick

Wick

HOLLOWED OUT *left*
The most basic form of lamp is a hollowed-out stone. This one came from the Shetland Islands, and was used during the last century. But similar examples have been found in the caves at Lascaux, France, dating from about 15,000 years ago.

MOULDS
Candles have been made in moulds since the 15th century. They made candle-making easier, but were not widely used until the process was mechanized in the 19th century.

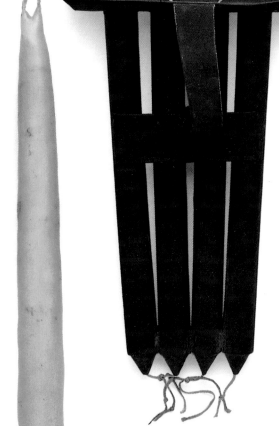

LIGHTS OUT
Conical snuffers were often used to put out candles. There was no smell and little risk of being burned.

DRY AS TINDER
Before the introduction of matches, tinder boxes were used to light fires and lamps. A spark was made by striking a flint (the striker) against a piece of metal (the steel). Some dry material (the tinder) in the box would catch fire.

Handle

Tinder

Steel

Lid

Candle holder

Striker

Tinder box

Cover to put out fire

TRIMMING THE WICK
With the appearance of more sophisticated oil lamps, elaborate tools were made to cut the wicks. This wick trimmer clips the wick and flicks the debris into the container.

CANDLE POWER *above*
A single candle produces only a little light – one candle power.

PROTECTOR
Lanterns were used to shield the flame from the wind and to reduce the risk of fire.

Handle to raise candle

SWEETNESS AND LIGHT
Another way to make a candle was to use wax collected from a beehive. This could be rolled into a cylinder shape.

ON THE STREETS *above*
This engraving shows the first candle street lamp being lit in Paris in 1667. The lamplighter had to climb a stepladder to reach the lantern.

TWISTER *left*
This candlestick has a spiral mechanism. You can twist it as the candle burns down, to keep the flame at the same level.

Timekeeping

Awareness of time was important as soon as people began to cultivate the land. But it was the astronomers of ancient Egypt, some 3,000 years ago, who used the regular movement of the Sun through the sky to tell time more accurately. The Egyptian shadow clock was a sundial, indicating time by the position of a shadow falling across markers. Other early devices for telling time depended on the regular burning of a candle, or the flow of water through a small hole. The first mechanical clocks used the regular rocking of a metal rod, called a foliot, to regulate the movement of a hand around a dial. Later clocks use pendulums, which move back and forth. The escapement ensures that this regular movement is transmitted to the gears which drive the hands.

BOOK OF HOURS
Medieval books of hours, with pictures of peasant life in the different months, show how important the time of the year was to people working on the land. This is the illustration for the month of March, from the *Très Riches Heures* of the Duc du Berry.

PLUMBLINE
The ancient Egyptian merkhet was used to observe the movement of certain stars across the sky, allowing the hours of the night to be calculated. This one belonged to an astronomer-priest of about 600 B.C. called Bes.

COLUMN DIAL
This small ivory sundial has two gnomons (pointers), one for summer, one for winter.

Folding gnomon

Holes to take pin

Cover

String gnomon

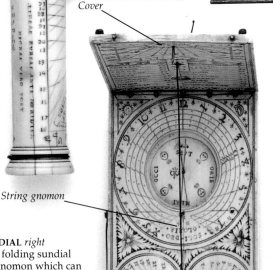

HANDY SUNDIAL *right*
This German folding sundial has a string gnomon which can be adjusted for different latitudes. The small dials show Italian and Babylonian hours. The dial also indicates the length of the day and the position of the sun in the zodiac.

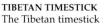

TIBETAN TIMESTICK
The Tibetan timestick relied on the shadow cast by a pin through an upright rod. The pin would be placed in different positions according to the time of the year.

WATER CLOCK
Su Sung's water clock, built in 1088, was housed in a tower 10 m (35 ft) high. Its water wheel paused after each bucket filled, marking intervals of time. Gears conveyed the motion to a globe.

Adjustable weights

LANTERN CLOCK
The moving balance bar can be seen on this Japanese lantern clock. The clock was regulated by moving small weights along the bar. The clock has only one hand indicating the hour. Minute hands were uncommon before the 1650s, when Dutch scientist Christiaan Huygens made a more accurate clock regulated by a swinging pendulum.

BRACKET CLOCK *below*
This type of clock was made in the 17th century. This example was made by the famous English clockmaker, Thomas Tompion. It has dials to regulate the mechanism and to select striking or silent operation.

CHRISTAAN HUYGENS
This Dutch scientist made the first practical pendulum clock in the mid 17th century.

VERGE WATCH
Until the 16th century, clocks were powered by falling weights, and could not be moved about. The use of a coiled spring to drive the hands meant that portable clocks and watches could be made, but they were not very accurate. This example is from the 17th century.

BALANCE-SPRING WATCH
Christiaan Huygens introduced the balance spring in 1675. It allowed much more accurate watch movements to be made. Thomas Tompion, the maker of this watch, introduced the balance spring to England, giving that country a leading position in watchmaking.

SANDS OF TIME *above*
The sandglass was probably first used in the Middle Ages, around 1300 A.D., although this is a much later example. Sand flowed through a narrow hole between two glass bulbs. When all the sand was in the lower bulb, a fixed time had passed.

Harnessing power

Since the dawn of history, people have looked for sources of power to make work easier and more efficient. First they made human muscle power more effective with the use of machines such as cranes and treadmills. It was soon realized that the muscle power of animals such as horses, mules, and oxen, was much greater than that of humans. Animals were trained to pull heavy loads and work in treadmills. Other useful sources of power came from wind and water. The first sailing ships were made in Egypt about 5,000 years ago. The Romans used water mills for grinding corn during the 1st century B.C. Water power remained important and is still widely used today. Windmills spread westward across Europe in the Middle Ages, when people began to look for a more efficient way of grinding corn.

MUSCLE POWER
Dogs are still used in arctic regions to pull sleds, although elsewhere in the world the horse was the most common working animal. Horses were also used to turn machinery such as grindstones and pumps.

POST MILL
Many of the earliest windmills were post mills. The whole mill could turn about its central post in order to face into the wind. Made of timber, many post mills were quite fragile and could blow over in a storm.

HAUL AWAY!
This 15th-century crane in Bruges, Belgium, was worked by men walking on a treadmill. It is shown lifting wine kegs. Other simple machines, such as the lever and pulley, were the mainstay of early industry. It is said that, around 250 B.C., the Greek scientist Archimedes could move a large ship single-handed using a system of pulleys. It is not known exactly how he did this.

Tail pole

THE FIRST WATER WHEELS
From around 70 B.C. we have records of the Romans using two types of water wheel to grind corn. In the undershot wheel, the water passes beneath the wheel; in the overshot wheel, the water flows over the top. The latter can be more efficient, using the weight of the water held on the blades.

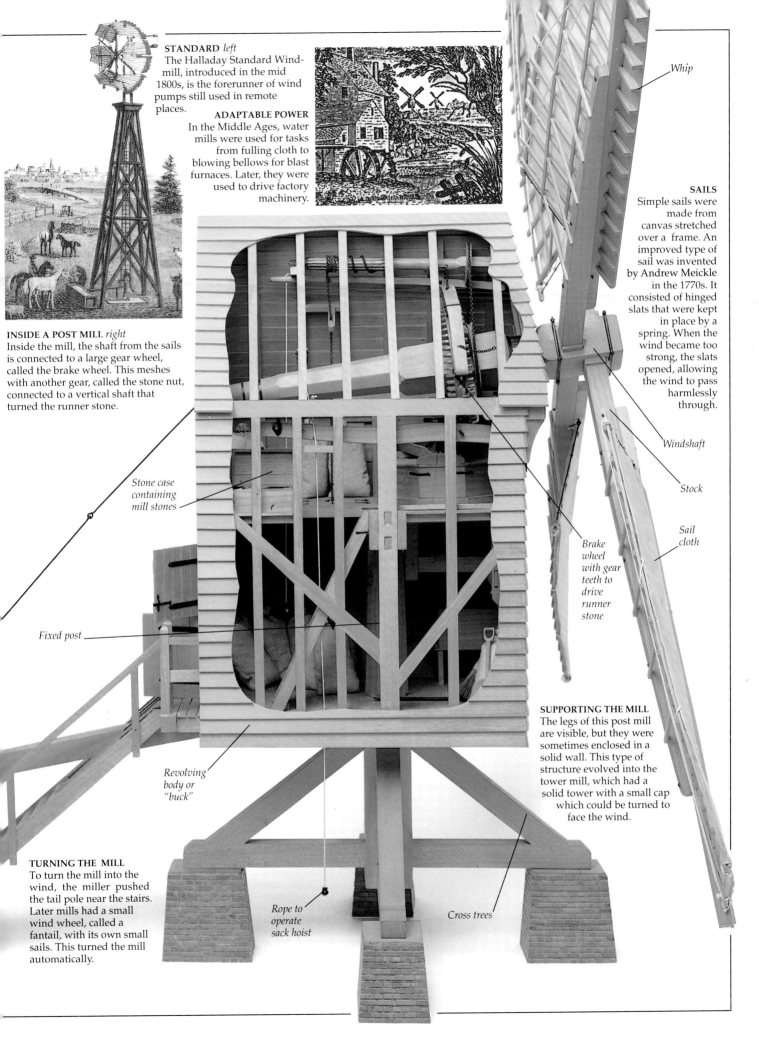

STANDARD *left*
The Halladay Standard Windmill, introduced in the mid 1800s, is the forerunner of wind pumps still used in remote places.

ADAPTABLE POWER
In the Middle Ages, water mills were used for tasks from fulling cloth to blowing bellows for blast furnaces. Later, they were used to drive factory machinery.

INSIDE A POST MILL *right*
Inside the mill, the shaft from the sails is connected to a large gear wheel, called the brake wheel. This meshes with another gear, called the stone nut, connected to a vertical shaft that turned the runner stone.

Stone case containing mill stones

Fixed post

Revolving body or "buck"

TURNING THE MILL
To turn the mill into the wind, the miller pushed the tail pole near the stairs. Later mills had a small wind wheel, called a fantail, with its own small sails. This turned the mill automatically.

Rope to operate sack hoist

Cross trees

Whip

SAILS
Simple sails were made from canvas stretched over a frame. An improved type of sail was invented by Andrew Meickle in the 1770s. It consisted of hinged slats that were kept in place by a spring. When the wind became too strong, the slats opened, allowing the wind to pass harmlessly through.

Windshaft

Stock

Sail cloth

Brake wheel with gear teeth to drive runner stone

SUPPORTING THE MILL
The legs of this post mill are visible, but they were sometimes enclosed in a solid wall. This type of structure evolved into the tower mill, which had a solid tower with a small cap which could be turned to face the wind.

Printing

This early Japanese wooden printing block has a complete passage of text carved into a single block of wood.

BEFORE PRINTING BEGAN, each copy of every book had to be written out laboriously by hand. This made books rare and expensive. The first people to print books were the Chinese and Japanese in the sixth century. Wooden, clay, or ivory blocks were used on which characters and pictures were engraved. When a paper sheet was pressed against the inked block, the characters were printed by the raised areas of the engraving. This is known as letterpress printing. The greatest advance in printing was the invention of movable type – single letters on small individual blocks that could be set in lines and re-used. This also began in China, in the 11th century. Movable type was first used in Europe in the 15th century. The most important pioneer was Johannes Gutenberg, who invented typecasting – a method of making large amounts of accurate movable type cheaply and quickly. After Gutenberg's work in the late 1430s, printing with movable type spread quickly across Europe.

EARLY TYPE
Blocks with one character were first used in China in about 1040. These are casts of early Turkish types.

PUNCHES
Gutenberg used a hard metal punch, carved with a letter. This was hammered into a soft metal to make a mould.

Letter stamped in metal

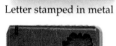

IN GOOD SHAPE
Each matrix bore the impression of a letter or symbol.

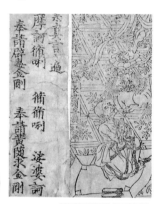

FROM THE ORIENT
This early Chinese book was printed with wooden blocks, each of which bore a single character.

POURING HOT METAL
A ladle was used to pour molten metal, a mixture of tin, lead, and antimony into the mould to form a piece of type.

THE GUTENBERG BIBLE
In 1455 Gutenberg produced the first large printed book, a Bible which is still regarded as a masterpiece of the printer's art.

TYPE MOULD
The matrix was placed in the bottom of a mould like this. The mould was then closed and the molten metal was poured in through the top. The sides were opened to release the type.

Mould inserted here

Spring to hold mould closed

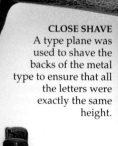

Screw to secure blade

Metal blade

CLOSE SHAVE
A type plane was used to shave the backs of the metal type to ensure that all the letters were exactly the same height.

REVERSED WORDS *above*
Early printers arranged type into words on a small tray called a composing stick. The letters have to be arranged from right to left, because the printed impression is the mirror image of the type.

SPACING THE WORDS *below*
The type on this modern composing stick shows how you could adjust the length of the line by inserting small pieces of metal between the words. These would not print because they are lower than the raised type.

Piece of type

Spacer

How the traditional composing stick was held in the hand

Adjustable grip to set length of line

Compositor setting type by hand

GUTENBERG'S WORKSHOP
About 1438, the German goldsmith, Johannes Gutenberg, invented a method of making type of individual letters from molten metal. Printers can be seen setting type and using the press in his workshop. Printed pages are hanging up for the ink to dry.

Screw locks type in place

Type forming a single page

HELD TIGHT
When the type was complete it was placed in a metal frame called a chase. The type is locked in place with pieces of wood or metal to make the forme. The forme is then placed in the printing press, inked, and printed.

Optical inventions

THE SCIENCE OF OPTICS is based on the fact that light rays are bent, or refracted, when they pass from one medium to another (for example, from air to glass). The way in which curved pieces of glass (or lenses) refract light was known to the Chinese in the 10th century A.D. In Europe in the 13th and 14th centuries the properties of lenses began to be used for improving vision, and spectacles appeared. For thousands of years, people used mirrors (made at first of shiny metals) to see their faces. But it was not until the 17th century that more powerful optical instruments, capable of magnifying very small items and bringing distant objects into clearer focus, began to be made. Developments at this time included the telescope, which appeared at the beginning of the century, and the microscope, invented around 1650.

IN THE DISTANCE
The telescope must have been invented many times - whenever someone put two lenses together like this and realised they could make distant objects look larger.

GLASS EYES?
Convex (outward-curving) lenses were known in 10th-century China, but the use of lenses for reading glasses and to make spectacles for the long-sighted probably began in Europe. These 17th-century reading glasses use convex lenses.

BLURRED VISION
Spectacles, pairs of lenses for correcting sight defects, have been in use for over 700 years. At first they were used only for reading and, like the ones being sold by this early optician, were perched on the nose when needed. Spectacles for correcting short-sightedness were first made in the 1450s.

17th-century spectacles

17th-century glass was often coloured

Leather-covered tube

Lens cap

STARGAZING
The celebrated Italian scientist and astronomer Galileo Galilei pioneered the use of refracting telescopes to study the heavens. This is a replica of one of Galileo's earliest instruments. It has a convex lens at the front and a concave (inward-curving) lens at the viewing end.

Concave lens

Convex lens

COLOURING THE VIEW
Early refracting telescopes, such as this 18th-century English model, produced images with blurred, coloured edges, because their lenses bent the different colours of light by different amounts. In 1729, Chester Moor Hall had a main lens made by putting together two lenses made of different sorts of glass. The colour distortion of one lens was counteracted by the other's.

Eyepiece lens

Objective lens

**ANTONI VAN LEEUWENHOEK
(1632-1723)** *left*
Dutchman Leeuwenhoek taught himself to grind lenses and made simple microscopes with a tiny lens in a metal frame. Obtaining magnifications of up to 280 times, he was one of the first to study the miniature natural world, and described "very little and odd animalcules" in drops of pond water.

COMPOUND INTEREST *above*
The compound microscope has not one but two lenses. The main lens magnifies the object, and the eyepiece lens enlarges the magnified image.

Lens cap

Lens cap

**ON
REFLECTION**
The reflecting telescope uses a mirror lens. This avoids the problem of colour distortion and the need for long focal-length lenses and long viewing tubes. This version has two mirrors and an eyepiece lens.

Geared focusing mechanism

ON THE LEVEL
A quadrant and plumb line are fitted to this 17th-century telescope. They help the astronomer work out the altitude of an object in the sky.

PEEPING TOM
Jealousy glasses were sometimes used by the 18th-century gentry for keeping an eye on one another. A mirror in the tube reflects the light rays so that you could look to one side when it seemed that you were looking straight ahead.

Eyepiece

18th-century pocket telescope

Focus adjuster

**EYE-EYE,
WHAT'S THAT?**
Simple binoculars, like these 19th-century opera glasses decorated with mother-of-pearl and enamel, consist of two telescopes mounted side-by-side. Prism binoculars had been invented by 1880. The prism, a wedge of glass, "folded" the light rays to shorten the length of the tube and allow greater magnification in a smaller instrument.

Calculating

PEOPLE HAVE ALWAYS counted and calculated, but calculating became very important when the buying and selling of goods began. Apart from fingers, the first aids to counting and calculating were small pebbles, used to represent the numbers from one to ten. The Mesopotamians, about 5,000 years ago, made several straight furrows in the ground into which the pebbles were placed. Simple calculations could be done by moving the pebbles from one furrow to another. Later, in China and Japan, the abacus was used in the same way, with its rows of beads representing hundreds, tens, and units. The next advances did not come until much later, with the invention of calculating aids like logarithms, the slide rule and basic mechanical calculators in the 17th century A.D.

Upper beads are five times the value of lower beads

USING AN ABACUS
Experienced users can calculate at great speed with an abacus. As a result, this method of calculation has remained popular in China and Japan – even in the age of the electronic calculator.

POCKET CALCULATOR
The ancient Romans used a similar abacus to the Chinese. It had one bead on each rod in the upper part; these beads represented five times the value of the lower beads. This is a replica of a small Roman hand abacus made of brass.

THE ABACUS
In the Chinese abacus, there are five beads on the lower parts of each rod, representing 1, and two beads on the upper part, representing 5. The user moves the beads to perform calculations. The abacus is still used in China today.

HARD BARGAIN
Making quick calculations became important in the Middle Ages, when merchants began to trade all around Europe. The merchant in this Flemish painting is adding up the weight of a number of gold coins.

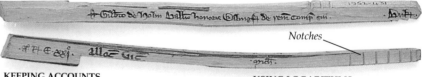

Notches

KEEPING ACCOUNTS
On tally sticks, the figures were cut into the stick in the form of a series of notches. The stick was then split in two along its length, through the notches, so each person involved in the deal had a record.

USING LOGARITHMS
To multiply two numbers, it is only necessary to add their logarithms. The slide rule, with its adjacent scales of numbers, works on this principle.

Parallel scales

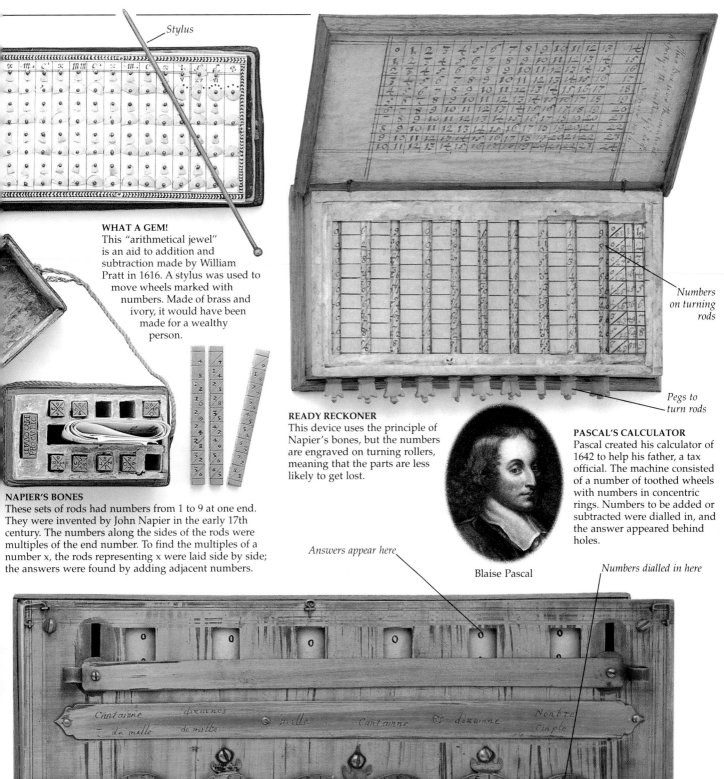

Stylus

WHAT A GEM!
This "arithmetical jewel" is an aid to addition and subtraction made by William Pratt in 1616. A stylus was used to move wheels marked with numbers. Made of brass and ivory, it would have been made for a wealthy person.

Numbers on turning rods

READY RECKONER
This device uses the principle of Napier's bones, but the numbers are engraved on turning rollers, meaning that the parts are less likely to get lost.

Pegs to turn rods

NAPIER'S BONES
These sets of rods had numbers from 1 to 9 at one end. They were invented by John Napier in the early 17th century. The numbers along the sides of the rods were multiples of the end number. To find the multiples of a number x, the rods representing x were laid side by side; the answers were found by adding adjacent numbers.

PASCAL'S CALCULATOR
Pascal created his calculator of 1642 to help his father, a tax official. The machine consisted of a number of toothed wheels with numbers in concentric rings. Numbers to be added or subtracted were dialled in, and the answer appeared behind holes.

Blaise Pascal

Answers appear here

Numbers dialled in here

The steam engine

Hero of Alexandria's steam engine

THE POWER DEVELOPED BY STEAM has fascinated people for hundreds of years. During the first century A.D., Greek scientists realized that steam contained energy that could possibly be used by people. But the ancient Greeks did not use steam power to drive machinery. The first steam engines were designed at the end of the 17th century by engineers such as the Marquis of Worcester and Thomas Savery. Savery's engine was intended to be used for pumping water out of mines. The first really practical steam engine was designed by Thomas Newcomen, whose first engine appeared in 1712. Scottish instrument maker James Watt improved the steam engine still further. His engines condensed steam outside the main cylinder. By dispensing with the need alternately to heat and cool the cylinder, this saved heat. The engines also used steam to force the piston down, to increase efficiency. The new engines soon became a major source of power for factories and mines. Later developments included the more compact, high-pressure engine, which was used in locomotives and ships.

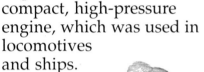

Parallel motion

Piston rod

Cylinder

GREEK STEAM POWER
Some time during the 1st century A.D., the Greek scientist Hero of Alexandria invented the æolipile - a simple steam engine that used the principle of jet propulsion. Water was boiled inside the sphere, and steam came out of bent jets attached to it. This made the ball turn around. The device was not used for any practical purpose.

Valve chest

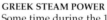

"Eduction pipe" to condenser

Air pump

Cistern containing condenser and air pump

PUMPING WATER
Thomas Savery (c. 1650–1715) patented a machine for pumping water from mines in 1698. Steam from a boiler passed into a pair of vessels. The steam was then condensed back into water, sucking water from the mine below. Using stop cocks and valves, steam pressure was then directed to push the water up a vertical outlet pipe. Thomas Newcomen (1663–1729) produced an improved engine in 1712.

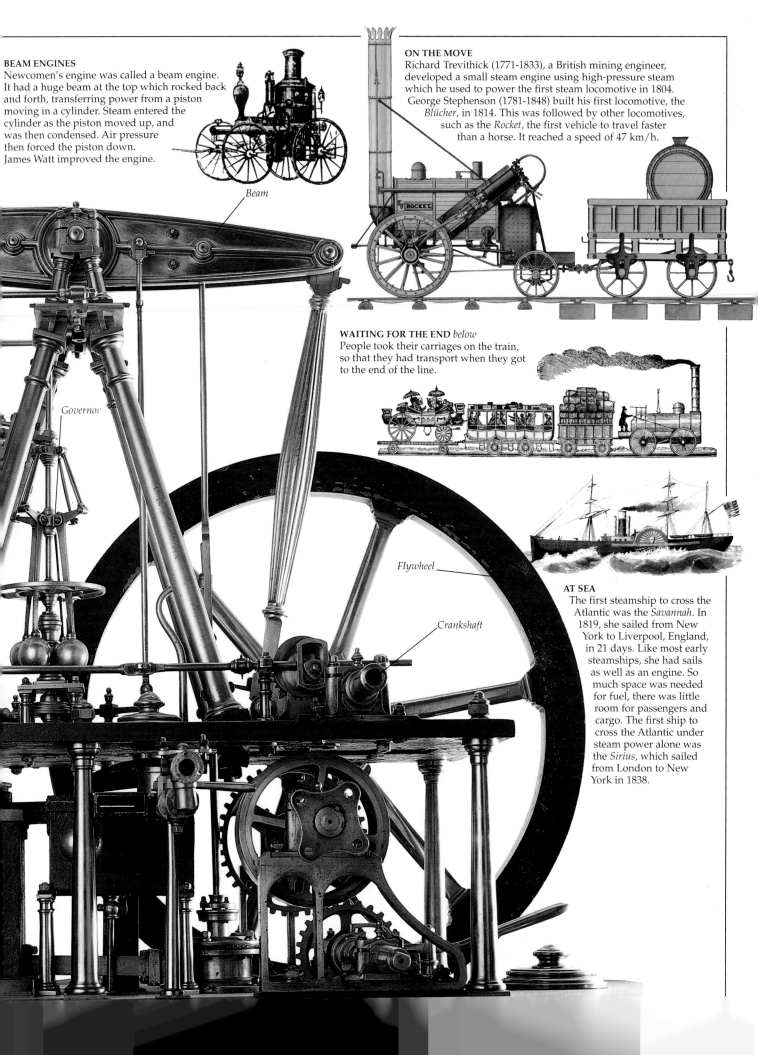

BEAM ENGINES
Newcomen's engine was called a beam engine. It had a huge beam at the top which rocked back and forth, transferring power from a piston moving in a cylinder. Steam entered the cylinder as the piston moved up, and was then condensed. Air pressure then forced the piston down. James Watt improved the engine.

Beam

Governor

Flywheel

Crankshaft

ON THE MOVE
Richard Trevithick (1771-1833), a British mining engineer, developed a small steam engine using high-pressure steam which he used to power the first steam locomotive in 1804. George Stephenson (1781-1848) built his first locomotive, the *Blücher*, in 1814. This was followed by other locomotives, such as the *Rocket*, the first vehicle to travel faster than a horse. It reached a speed of 47 km/h.

WAITING FOR THE END *below*
People took their carriages on the train, so that they had transport when they got to the end of the line.

AT SEA
The first steamship to cross the Atlantic was the *Savannah*. In 1819, she sailed from New York to Liverpool, England, in 21 days. Like most early steamships, she had sails as well as an engine. So much space was needed for fuel, there was little room for passengers and cargo. The first ship to cross the Atlantic under steam power alone was the *Sirius*, which sailed from London to New York in 1838.

Navigation and surveying

THE MORE PEOPLE TRAVELLED by boat, the more important the skills of navigation became. Navigation probably originated on the Nile and Euphrates about 5,000 years ago, when the Egyptians and Babylonians established trading routes. The Egyptians also pioneered surveying, essential for creating large buildings such as the pyramids. Navigation and surveying are related, because both deal with measuring angles and calculating long distances. From around 500 B.C., first the Greeks, then the Arabs and Indians, established astronomy, geometry and trigonometry as sciences and created such instruments as the astrolabe and compass.

Understanding the movements of heavenly bodies and the relationship between angles and distances, medieval seafarers were able to create a system of longitude and latitude for finding their way at sea without reference to landmarks. The Romans pioneered the widespread use of accurate surveying instruments and Renaissance architects added the theodolite, our most important surveying tool.

Chinese mariner's compass

English compass

IN THE RIGHT DIRECTION
Magnetic compasses were used in Europe by about A.D.1200 but the Chinese are thought to have noticed about 1,500 years before that a suspended piece of lodestone (a magnetic iron mineral) points North-South.

Handle

Stones suspended from crossed sticks set at right angles to one another

RIGHT ANGLE *above*
Early surveyor's instruments such as the Egyptian groma were useful only on flat terrain and for setting a limited range of angles. With the groma, distant objects were marked out against the position of the stones in a horizontal plane.

Central arm

STRETCHING IT OUT
Ropes, chains, tapes and rods have all been used for measuring distances. In about 1620, Edmund Gunter developed this type of metal chain for determining the area of plots of land. The chain is 20 m (66 ft) long, and is made of 100 links. Markers are placed at regular intervals.

Brass marker

OCTANT
In the 1730s English seafarer John Hadley invented the octant. This version is from about 1750. It enabled navigators to measure the altitude of the Sun, Moon, or stars so that they could find their latitude.

Chain link

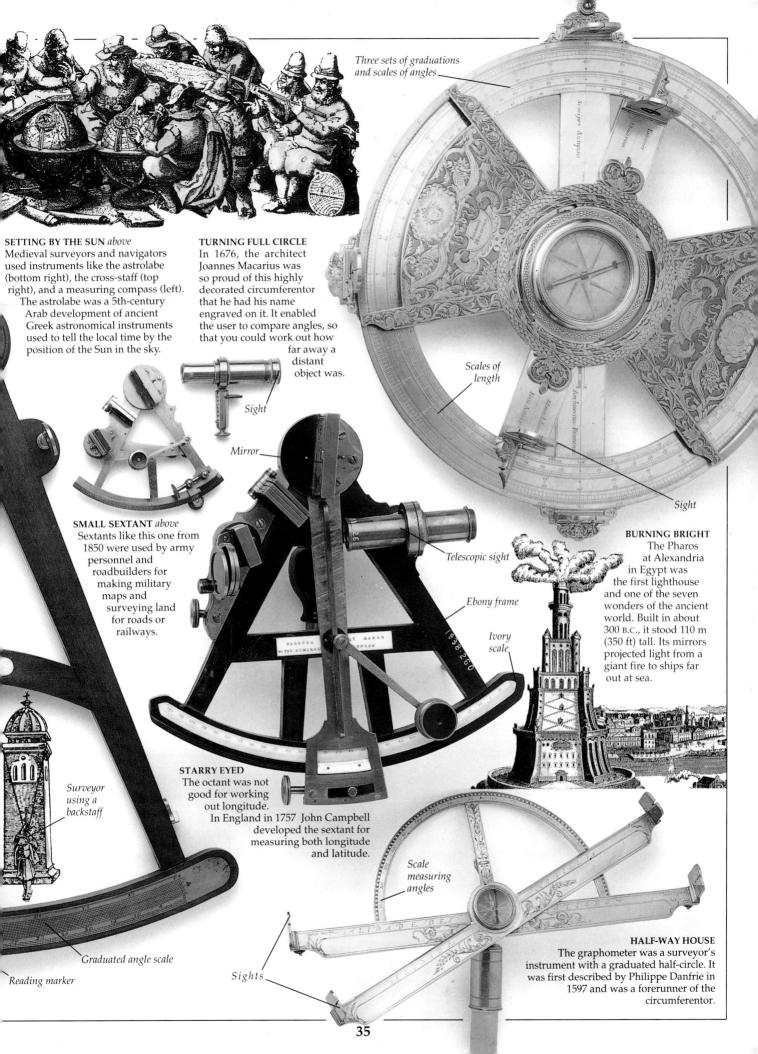

SETTING BY THE SUN *above*
Medieval surveyors and navigators used instruments like the astrolabe (bottom right), the cross-staff (top right), and a measuring compass (left). The astrolabe was a 5th-century Arab development of ancient Greek astronomical instruments used to tell the local time by the position of the Sun in the sky.

TURNING FULL CIRCLE
In 1676, the architect Joannes Macarius was so proud of this highly decorated circumferentor that he had his name engraved on it. It enabled the user to compare angles, so that you could work out how far away a distant object was.

Three sets of graduations and scales of angles

Scales of length

Sight

Sight

Mirror

Telescopic sight

Ebony frame

Ivory scale

SMALL SEXTANT *above*
Sextants like this one from 1850 were used by army personnel and roadbuilders for making military maps and surveying land for roads or railways.

BURNING BRIGHT
The Pharos at Alexandria in Egypt was the first lighthouse and one of the seven wonders of the ancient world. Built in about 300 B.C., it stood 110 m (350 ft) tall. Its mirrors projected light from a giant fire to ships far out at sea.

Surveyor using a backstaff

STARRY EYED
The octant was not good for working out longitude. In England in 1757 John Campbell developed the sextant for measuring both longitude and latitude.

Scale measuring angles

Graduated angle scale

Reading marker

Sights

HALF-WAY HOUSE
The graphometer was a surveyor's instrument with a graduated half-circle. It was first described by Philippe Danfrie in 1597 and was a forerunner of the circumferentor.

Spinning and weaving

Early people used animal skins to help them keep warm, but, about 10,000 years ago, people learned how to make cloth. Wool, cotton, flax, or hemp was first spun into a thin thread, using a spindle. The thread was then woven into a fabric. The earliest weaving machines probably consisted of little more than a pair of sticks that held a set of parallel threads, called the warp, whilst the cross-thread, called the weft, was inserted. Later machines, called looms, had rods that separated the threads to allow the weft to be inserted more easily. A piece of wood, called the shuttle, holding a spool of thread, was passed between the separated threads. The basic principles of spinning and weaving have stayed the same until the present day, although during the industrial revolution of the 18th century many ways were found of automating the processes. With new machines such as the spinning mule, many threads could be spun at the same time and, with the help of devices like the flying shuttle, broad pieces of cloth could be woven at great speed.

CLOTHMAKING IN THE MIDDLE AGES
By about A.D. 1300, an improved loom was introduced to Europe from India. Called the horizontal loom, it had a framework of string or wire to separate the warp threads. The shuttle was passed across the loom by hand.

ANCIENT SPINDLE
Spindles like this were turned by hand to twist the fibres, and allowed to hang so that the fibres were drawn in to a thread. This example was found in 1921 at the ancient Egyptian site at Tel el Amarna.

Drive thread

Wool

Wooden wheel

SPINNING AT HOME
The spinning wheel, which was introduced to Europe from India about A.D. 1200, speeded up the spinning process. The wheel was turned by the right hand while a sliver of wool, which was attached to the yarn already spun, was drawn out with the left.

SPINNING WHEEL
This type of spinning wheel, called the great wheel, was used in homes across Europe until about 200 years ago. Spinning wheels like this produced a fine yarn of even thickness.

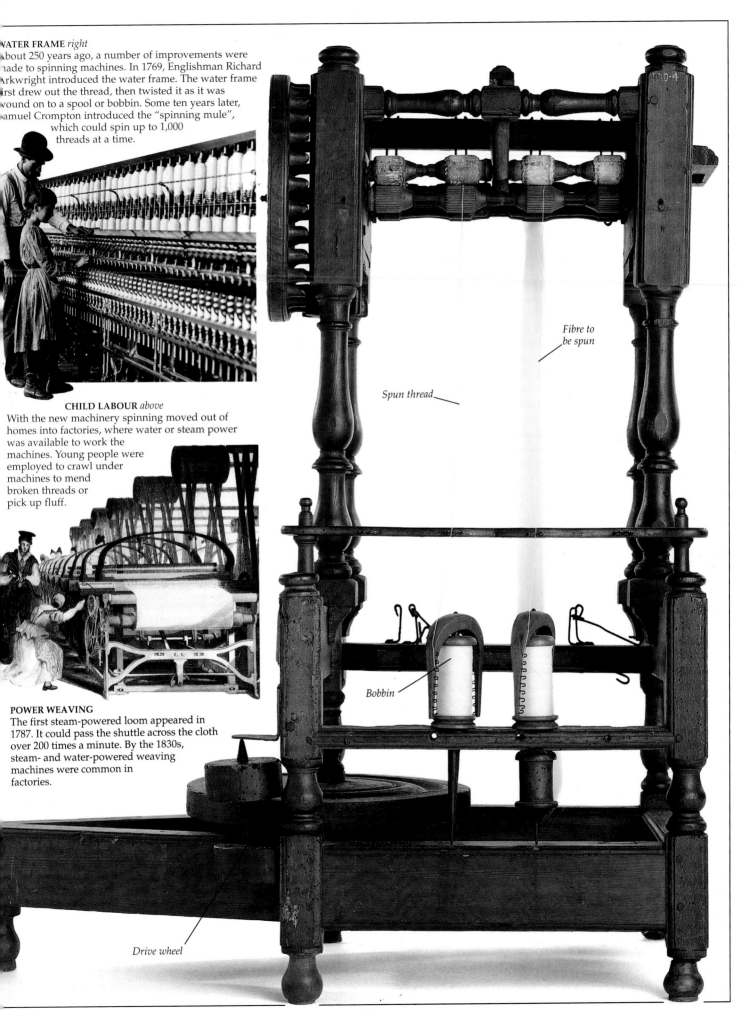

WATER FRAME *right*

About 250 years ago, a number of improvements were made to spinning machines. In 1769, Englishman Richard Arkwright introduced the water frame. The water frame first drew out the thread, then twisted it as it was wound on to a spool or bobbin. Some ten years later, Samuel Crompton introduced the "spinning mule", which could spin up to 1,000 threads at a time.

CHILD LABOUR *above*

With the new machinery spinning moved out of homes into factories, where water or steam power was available to work the machines. Young people were employed to crawl under machines to mend broken threads or pick up fluff.

POWER WEAVING

The first steam-powered loom appeared in 1787. It could pass the shuttle across the cloth over 200 times a minute. By the 1830s, steam- and water-powered weaving machines were common in factories.

Fibre to be spun

Spun thread

Bobbin

Drive wheel

37

Batteries

Over 2,000 years ago, the Greek scientist Thales produced small electric sparks by rubbing a cloth against amber, a yellow resin formed from the sap of long-dead trees. But it was a long time before people succeeded in harnessing this power to produce a battery – a device for producing a steady flow of electricity. It was in 1800 that Alessandro Volta (1745-1827) published details of the first battery. Volta's battery produced electricity using the chemical reaction between certain solutions and metal electrodes. Other scientists, such as John Frederic Daniell (1790-1845), improved Volta's design by using different materials for the electrodes. Today's batteries follow the same basic design but use modern materials.

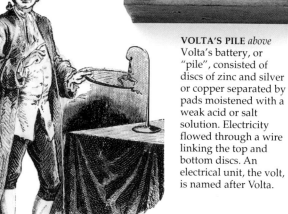

Metal electrodes

Fabric pads

VOLTA'S PILE *above*
Volta's battery, or "pile", consisted of discs of zinc and silver or copper separated by pads moistened with a weak acid or salt solution. Electricity flowed through a wire linking the top and bottom discs. An electrical unit, the volt, is named after Volta.

LIGHTNING FLASH
In 1752, American inventor Benjamin Franklin flew a kite in a thunderstorm. Electricity flowed down the wet line and produced a small spark, showing that lightning bolts were huge electric sparks.

ANIMAL ELECTRICITY
Luigi Galvani (1737-1798) found that the legs of dead frogs twitched when they were touched with metal rods. He thought the legs contained "animal electricity". Volta suggested a different explanation. Animals do produce electricity, but the twitching of the frog's legs was probably caused by the metal rods and the moisture in the legs forming a simple cell.

Space filled with acid or solution

BUCKET CHEMISTRY
To produce higher voltages, and thus larger currents, many cells, each consisting of a pair of electrodes of different metals, were connected together. The common "voltaic" cell consists of copper and zinc electrodes immersed in weak acid. The English inventor Cruikshank created this "trough" battery in 1800. The metal plates were soldered back-to-back and cemented into slots in a wooden case. The case was then filled with a dilute acid or a solution of ammonium chloride.

Zinc plate *Handles for lifting out zinc plates* *Copper plate*

DIPPING IN, DRYING OUT
In about 1807, W. H. Wollaston, an English chemist, created a battery like this. Zinc plates were fixed between the arms of U-shaped copper plates, so that both sides of the zinc were used. The zinc plates were lifted out of the electrolyte to save zinc when the battery was not in use.

RELIABLE ELECTRICITY

The Daniell cell was the first reliable source of electricity. It produced a steady voltage over a considerable time. The cell has a copper electrode immersed in copper sulphate solution, and a zinc electrode in sulphuric acid. The liquids are kept separate by a porous pot.

Porous pot

Copper can acting as electrode

Terminal

HARVEY & PEAK,
Reappointment to the Royal Institution of Gt. Britain
Scientific Instrument Manufacturers
And ELECTRICIANS,
5, SANDRINGHAM BUILDINGS,
CHARING CROSS ROAD,
LONDON, W.C.

RECHARGEABLE BATTERY

The French scientist Gaston Planté was a pioneer of the lead-acid accumulator, which can be recharged when it runs down. It has electrodes of lead and lead oxide in strong sulphuric acid.

Zinc rod electrode

GASSNER CELL *left*

Chemist Carl Gassner developed a pioneering type of "dry" cell. He used a zinc case as the negative (-) electrode, and a carbon rod as the positive (+) electrode. In between them was a paste of ammonium chloride solution and Plaster of Paris.

HUBBLE BUBBLE *right*

Some early batteries used concentrated nitric acid but they gave off poisonous fumes. To avoid such hazards, the bichromate cell was developed in the 1850s. It used a glass flask filled with chromic acid. Zinc and carbon plates were used as electrodes.

POWERPACKS *left*

The so-called "dry" cell has a moist paste electrolyte inside a zinc container which acts as one electrode. The other electrode is manganese dioxide, connected via a carbon rod. Small modern batteries use a variety of materials for the electrodes. Mercury batteries were the first long-life dry cells. Some batteries use lithium, the lightest of metals. They have a very long life and are therefore used in heart pacemakers.

EVER READY
MADE IN BRITAIN
PATENT No. 536869
B103

EVER READY
UNIT
CELL
U2

VIDOR
G52
ETERNACELL
LITHIUM

VIDOR
G8/1
ETERNACELL
LITHIUM

Photography

THE INVENTION OF PHOTOGRAPHY made accurate images of any object rapidly available for the first time. It sprang from a combination of optics (see p. 28) and chemistry. The projection of the Sun's image on a screen had been explored by Arab astronomers in the 9th century A.D., and by the Chinese before them. By the 16th century, Italian artists such as Canaletto were using lenses and a camera obscura to help them make accurate drawings. In 1725 a German professor, Johann Heinrich Schulze, showed that the darkening of silver nitrate solution when exposed to the Sun was caused by light, not heat. In 1827, a light-sensitive material was coated on to a metal plate and a permanent visual record of an object was made.

IN THE BLACK BOX
The camera obscura (from the Latin for dark room) was at first just a darkened room or large box with a tiny opening at the front and a screen or wall at the back on to which images were projected. From the 16th century, a lens was used instead of the "pinhole".

CALOTYPE IMAGE
By 1841, Englishman William Henry Fox Talbot had developed the Calotype. This is an early example. It was an improved version of a process he had announced two years before, within days of Daguerre's announcement. It provided a negative image, from which positives could be printed.

The daguerreotype

Joseph Nicéphore Niepce took the first surviving photograph. In 1826, he coated a pewter plate with bitumen and exposed it in a camera. Where light struck, the bitumen hardened. The unhardened areas were then dissolved away to leave a visible image. In 1839, his one-time partner, Louis Jacques Daguerre, developed a superior photographic process, producing the daguerreotype.

Lens cover

EXPOSING THE PLATE *below*
In some daguerreotype cameras, the object was viewed through a hole in the back of the box. Then the photographic plate, protected by a cover, was slid into place. The lens cap and the cover were removed to expose the plate, then replaced.

Lens with focusing control

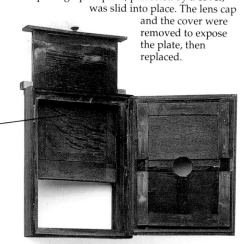

Plate holder

DAGUERREOTYPE IMAGE
A daguerreotype comprised a copper plate coated with silver and treated with iodine vapour to make it sensitive to light. It was exposed in the camera, then the image was developed by mercury vapour and fixed with a strong solution of ordinary salt.

Aperture rings

MAKING ADJUSTMENTS
Using screw-in lens fittings and different-size diaphragm rings to adjust the lens aperture, as on this folding daguerreotype camera of the 1840s, it became possible to photograph both close-up and distant objects in a variety of lighting conditions.

Lens and attachments

Folding daguerreotype camera

HEAVY LOADS
Enlargements could not be made with the early photographic processes, so for large pictures big glass plates were used. With a dark tent for inspecting wet-plates as they were exposed, water, chemicals, and plates, the equipment could weigh over 50 kg (110 lb).

The wet plate

From 1839 on, the pioneers of photography concentrated on the use of salts of silver as the light-sensitive material. In 1851 Frederick Scott Archer created a glass photographic plate more light-sensitive than its predecessors. It recorded negative images of fine detail with exposures of less than 30 seconds. The plate was coated with a chemical mix, put in the camera and exposed while still wet. It was a messy process, but gave excellent results.

Plate holder

Chemicals for wet-plate process

Wet-plate negative

CHEMICALS *above right*
A wet-plate consisted of a glass sheet coated with silver salts and a sticky material called collodion. It was usually developed with pyrogallic acid and fixed with sodium thiosulphate ("hypo"). Chemicals were dispensed from small bottles.

IN AND OUT OF VIEW
This wet-plate camera was mounted on a tripod. The rear section into which the photographic plate was inserted could slide in and out of the front lens section to increase or decrease the image size and produce a clear picture. Fine focusing was by means of a knob on the lens tube.

Modern photography

In the 1870s, dry gelatine-coated plates covered with extremely light-sensitive silver bromide were developed. Soon more sensitive paper allowed many prints to be made from a negative quickly and easily in a darkroom. In 1888, American George Eastman introduced a small, lightweight camera. It used film which came on a roll.

Film winder

PHOTOGRAPHY FOR ALL
In the early 1900s Eastman developed cheap Brownie box cameras such as this, and amateur photography was born. Each time a photo was taken, you would wind on the film ready for the next shot.

CANDID CAMERA *right*
By the 1920s, German optical instrument manufacturers such as Carl Zeiss were developing small precision cameras. This 1937 single-lens reflex (SLR) Exakta model is in many ways the forerunner of a whole generation of modern cameras.

Viewfinder

Film winder

Lens

SLR camera

ROLL-FILM
Eastman's early roll-film consisted of a long thin strip of paper from which the negative coating was stripped and put down on glass plates before printing. In 1889, celluloid roll-film came on the market. The light-sensitive emulsion was coated on to a see-through base so that the stripping process was eliminated.

Medical inventions

P EOPLE HAVE ALWAYS practised some form of medicine. Early peoples used herbs to cure illnesses, and prehistoric skulls have been found with round holes drilled through, probably with a trepan, a surgeon's circular saw. The ancient Greeks used this operation to relieve pressure on the brain after severe head injuries. The ancient Chinese practised acupuncture, inserting needles into one part of the body to relieve pain or the symptoms of disease in another part. But until well into the 19th century, a surgeon's instruments differed little from early ones – scalpels, forceps, various hooks, saws and other tools to perform amputations or to extract teeth. The first instruments used to determine the cause of illnesses were developed in Renaissance Europe following the pioneering anatomical work of scientists such as Leonardo da Vinci and Andreas Vesalius. In the 19th century, medicine developed quickly; much of the equipment still used in medicine and dentistry today, from stethoscopes to dental drills, were developed at this time.

PLUNGING IN
Syringes were first used in ancient India, China, and North Africa. Nowadays, syringes consist of a hollow glass or plastic barrel and a plunger. A syringe fitted with a blade was first used in about 1850 by French surgeon Charles Gabriel Pravaz to introduce fluids into veins.

Steam generator

Carbolic acid reservoir

Flexible rubber tube

Porcelain teeth

Mouthpiece placed over patient's mouth - has valves for breathing in and out

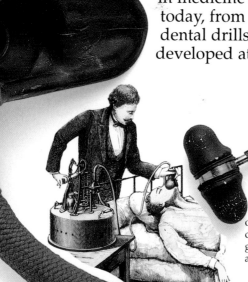

NUMBING PAIN
Before the discovery of anaesthetics in 1846, surgery was done while the patient was still conscious and capable of feeling pain. To numb pain, nitrous oxide (laughing gas), ether, or chloroform was used. The gases were inhaled via a face mask.

Coiled spring

Ivory lower plate

Drill bit

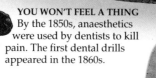

YOU WON'T FEEL A THING
By the 1850s, anaesthetics were used by dentists to kill pain. The first dental drills appeared in the 1860s.

DRILLING DOWN *right*
The Harrington "Erado" clockwork dental drill dates from about 1864. When fully wound, it worked for up to 2 minutes.

FIRM BITE *above*
The first full set of false teeth like those used today was made in France in the 1780s. This set of partial dentures, dates from about 1860.

SPRAY IT ON *left*
By 1865 Scottish surgeon Joseph Lister had developed an antiseptic carbolic steam spray. It created a mist of carbolic acid, intended to kill germs around the operation site. This version dates from about 1875.

THROUGH THE LOOKING TUBE *right*
Different types of endoscope, for viewing inside the body without surgery, were developed in the 19th century. This 1880s type used a candle as a light source.

Candle

DOWN THE TUBE
In 1819 French physician René Laënnec created a tube through which he could hear the patient's heartbeat.

Ivory earpiece

Speculum - placed in patient's ear

Funnel for concentrating light

Viewing lens

LISTENING IN
Laënnec's single-tube stethoscope was later developed into this 1855 version of the present-day design, with two earpieces. The stethoscope can be used to listen to the sounds made by the heart, lungs, or blood vessels, or to the heartbeat of a baby in the womb.

TAKING THE PULSE *left*
Physician William Harvey was, in the early 17th century, the first to show how blood circulated around the body. But it was not until much later that the link between the pulse, heart activity, and health was established.

Ether vapour outlet valve

Air inlet valve

Metal tubes (nowadays plastic ones), for transmitting the sounds

UNDER PRESSURE *above*
Blood pressure is measured by feeling the pulse and slowly applying a measured force to the skin until the pulse disappears. The instrument to do this was invented by Samuel von Basch and called a sphygmomanometer.

HOT UNDER THE COLLAR? *right*
These thermometers, from about 1865, were placed in the mouth (straight version) or under the armpit (curved-end type). Measuring the patient's temperature was not common practice until the early decades of this century.

Temperature scale in degrees Fahrenheit

Cone

Reservoir of mercury

Ether-soaked sponges

LIGHT-HEADED FEELING
In the 19th century, ether was used as an anaesthetic. The "Letheon" ether inhaler of 1847 comprised a glass jar filled with ether-soaked sponges through which air was drawn as the patient breathed in.

Kink in tube - to give good fit in armpit

HOLLOW SOUNDS
The disc-shaped sound collector on this 1830s stethoscope would have been used to listen to high-pitched sounds, like those made by the lungs, rather than low-pitched ones, which heartbeats produce.

The telephone

FOR CENTURIES, people have tried to send signals over long distances, using bonfires and flashing mirrors to carry messages. It was Frenchman Claude Chappe who in 1793 devised the word telegraph (literally, writing at a distance) to describe his message machine. Moving arms mounted on towertops signalled numbers and letters. Over the next 40 years, electric telegraphs were developed, and in 1876 Alexander Graham Bell invented the telephone, enabling speech to be sent along wires for the first time. Bell's work with the deaf led to an interest in how sounds are produced by vibrations in the air. His research on a device called the "harmonic telegraph" led him to discover that an electric current could be changed to resemble the vibrations made by a speaking voice. This was the principle on which his work on the telephone was based.

MAKING A CONNECTION
These two men are using early Edison equipment to make their telephone call. Two different arrangements – a modern-style receiver and a two-piece apparatus for speaking and listening, are clearly visible. All calls had to be made via the operator.

OPENING SPEECH
Alexander Graham Bell (1847–1922), developed the telephone after working with deaf people as a speech teacher. Here he is making the first call on the New York to Chicago line.

ALL-IN-ONE
Early models such as Bell's "Box telephone" of 1876–77 had a trumpet-like mouthpiece and earpiece combined. The instrument contains a membrane that vibrated when someone spoke into the mouthpiece. The vibrations created a varying electric current in a wire, and the receiver turned the varying current back into vibrations that you could hear.

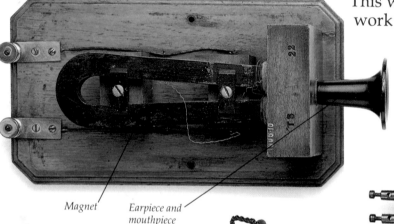

Magnet   *Earpiece and mouthpiece combined*

Wire coil   *Iron diaphragm*

EARPIECE
In this earpiece of about 1878 a fluctuating electric current passing through the wire coil made the iron diaphragm move to make sounds.

Telegraph

The forerunner of the telephone, the telegraph allowed signals to be sent along a wire. The first telegraphs were used on the railways to help keep track of trains. Later, telegraph wire linked major cities.

MESSAGE MACHINES
With the Morse key (left) you could send signals made up of short dots and long dashes. In the Cooke and Wheatstone system (right) the electric current made needles point at different letters.

DON'T HANG UP
In 1877 Thomas Edison developed different mouthpiece and earpiece units. Models such as this were hung from a special switch that disconnected the line on closing.

WIRED FOR SOUND
Some early telegraph cables used copper wires sheathed in glass. Overhead telegraph and phone wires used iron for strength.

EASY LISTENING
This wall-mounted telephone of 1879 was invented by Thomas Edison and has a microphone and receiver of his design. The user had to wind the handle while listening. A ring of the bell indicated an incoming call or a successful connection.

Earpiece

REPEAT THAT NUMBER
The earliest telephone exchanges were manual. One of the dozens of operators took your number and the number you wanted, and plugged in your line wire to complete the appropriate electrical circuit.

HANDSETS
By 1885 the transmitter and receiver had been combined to form a handset. At first this was metal, but by 1929 plastic handsets were common.

Mouthpiece

Mouthpiece

Hook for earpiece

IT'S A STICK-UP
Some candlestick-shaped phones of the 1920s and 1930s have a dial for calling numbers via an automatic exchange.

Transmitter containing carbon granules, compressed and released by sound waves to create an electric current of varying strength

Numbered dial

Earpiece

LONG DISTANCE CALL FOR YOU
"Cradle" telephones like this were popular by the 1890s. This one dates from 1937, by which time there was a transatlantic telephone service between London and New York.

Drawer for directory

45

Recording

SOUNDS WERE RECORDED for the first time in 1877 on an experimental machine which Thomas Edison (1847–1931) hoped would translate telephone calls into telegraph messages. It recorded the calls as indentations in a strip of paper passing under a stylus. Edison noticed that when he passed the indented paper through the machine again, he heard a faint echo of the original sound. This mechanical-acoustic method of recording continued until electrical systems appeared in the 1920s. Magnetic principles were used to develop tape recording systems. These received a commercial boost, first in 1935, with the development of magnetic plastic tape and then, in the 1960s, with the use of microelectronics (p. 62).

TWO IN ONE MACHINE
By 1877, Edison had created separate devices for recording and playing back. Sounds made into a horn caused its diaphragm to vibrate and its stylus to create indentations on a thin sheet of tinfoil wrapped around the recording drum. Putting the playback stylus and its diaphragm in contact with the foil and rotating the drum reproduced the sounds via a second diaphragm.

Mouthpiece (horn not shown)

Drive axle, threaded to move length of foil beneath fixed stylus

Brass drum - tinfoil wrapped round this

Cross-section showing needle on cylinder

Position of horn

Edison phonograph showing positions of needle and horn

PLAY IT AGAIN, SAM
The playback mechanism comprised a stylus made of steel in contact with a thin iron diaphragm. The wooden mount was flipped over so the stylus made close contact with the foil as it rotated. Vibrations from the foil were transferred to the diaphragm. As this moved in and out, it created sound waves.

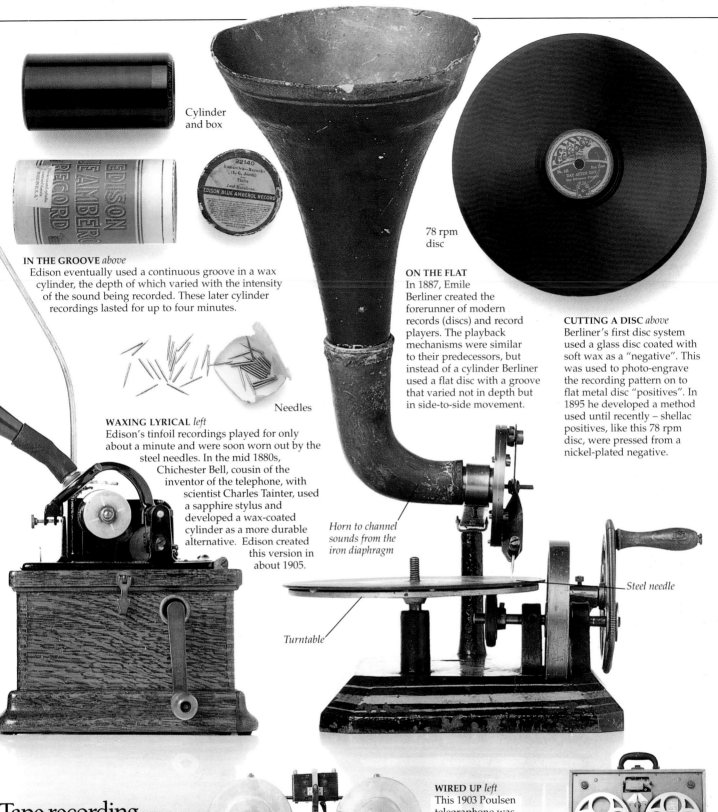

Cylinder
and box

78 rpm
disc

IN THE GROOVE *above*
Edison eventually used a continuous groove in a wax cylinder, the depth of which varied with the intensity of the sound being recorded. These later cylinder recordings lasted for up to four minutes.

ON THE FLAT
In 1887, Emile Berliner created the forerunner of modern records (discs) and record players. The playback mechanisms were similar to their predecessors, but instead of a cylinder Berliner used a flat disc with a groove that varied not in depth but in side-to-side movement.

CUTTING A DISC *above*
Berliner's first disc system used a glass disc coated with soft wax as a "negative". This was used to photo-engrave the recording pattern on to flat metal disc "positives". In 1895 he developed a method used until recently – shellac positives, like this 78 rpm disc, were pressed from a nickel-plated negative.

Needles

WAXING LYRICAL *left*
Edison's tinfoil recordings played for only about a minute and were soon worn out by the steel needles. In the mid 1880s, Chichester Bell, cousin of the inventor of the telephone, with scientist Charles Tainter, used a sapphire stylus and developed a wax-coated cylinder as a more durable alternative. Edison created this version in about 1905.

Horn to channel sounds from the iron diaphragm

Steel needle

Turntable

Tape recording

In 1898 Danish inventor Valdemar Poulsen produced the first magnetic recorder. Recordings were made on steel piano wire. In the 1930s, two German companies, Telefunken and I. G. Farben, developed a plastic tape coated with magnetic iron oxide, and this soon replaced steel wires and tapes.

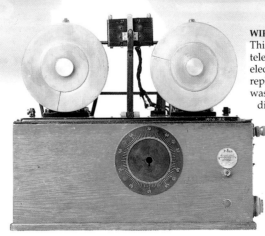

WIRED UP *left*
This 1903 Poulsen telegraphone was electrically driven and replayed. The machine was used primarily for dictation and telephone message work. The sounds were recorded on wire.

ON TAPE *above*
This tape recorder of about 1950 has three heads, one to erase previous recordings, one to record, and the third to replay.

The internal combustion engine

THE INTERNAL COMBUSTION ENGINE created a revolution in transport almost as great as that caused by the wheel. For the first time, a small, relatively efficient engine was available, leading to the production of vehicles from cars to aircraft. Inside an internal combustion engine a fuel burns (combusts) to produce power. The fuel burns inside a tube called a cylinder. Hot gases are formed during burning and these push a piston down the cylinder. The piston's movement produces the power to drive wheels or machinery. The first working internal combustion engine was built in 1859 by Belgian inventor Etienne Lenoir (1822–1900). It was powered by gas. The German engineer Nikolaus Otto (1832–1891) built an improved engine in 1876. This used four movements of the piston to produce its power, and became known as the four-stroke engine. The four-stroke engine was developed by Gottlieb Daimler and Karl Benz, leading to the production of the first automobile in 1886.

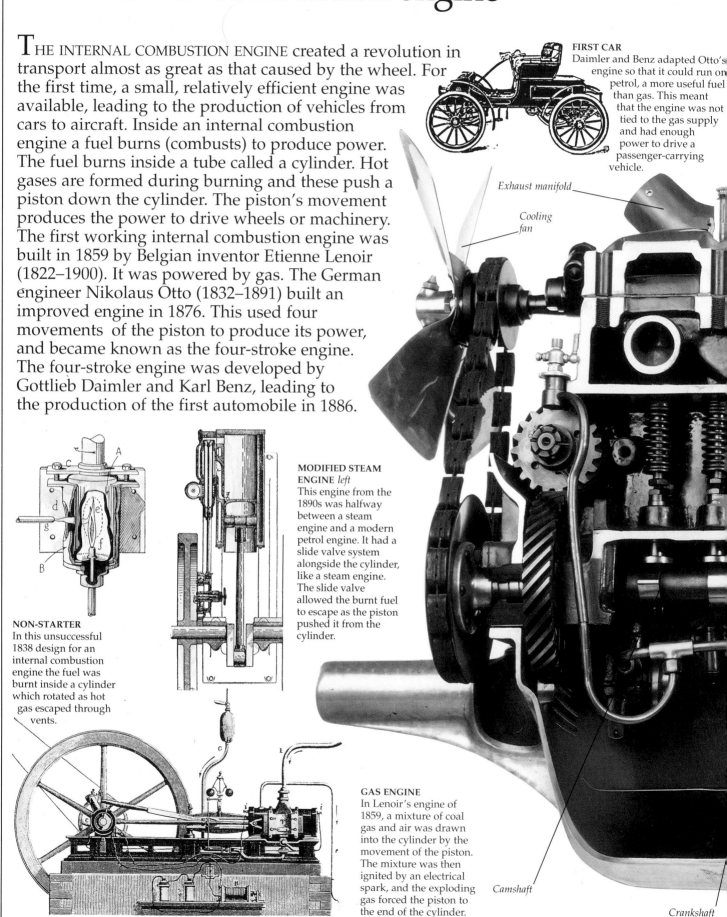

FIRST CAR
Daimler and Benz adapted Otto's engine so that it could run on petrol, a more useful fuel than gas. This meant that the engine was not tied to the gas supply and had enough power to drive a passenger-carrying vehicle.

Exhaust manifold

Cooling fan

MODIFIED STEAM ENGINE *left*
This engine from the 1890s was halfway between a steam engine and a modern petrol engine. It had a slide valve system alongside the cylinder, like a steam engine. The slide valve allowed the burnt fuel to escape as the piston pushed it from the cylinder.

NON-STARTER
In this unsuccessful 1838 design for an internal combustion engine the fuel was burnt inside a cylinder which rotated as hot gas escaped through vents.

GAS ENGINE
In Lenoir's engine of 1859, a mixture of coal gas and air was drawn into the cylinder by the movement of the piston. The mixture was then ignited by an electrical spark, and the exploding gas forced the piston to the end of the cylinder.

Camshaft

Crankshaft

FOUR-STROKE CYCLE
During the induction stroke, the piston moves down, sucking the fuel-air mixture into the cylinder through the open inlet valve. During the compression stroke, the piston moves up to compress the mixture; the spark plug ignites the mixture at the top of the stroke. During the power stroke, the expanding burnt fuel pushes the piston down. During the exhaust stroke, the piston moves up, forcing the burnt fuel out through the open exhaust valve.

Induction   Compression   Power   Exhaust

CAR OF THE PEOPLE *right*
The 1908 Model T Ford was the first car to be mass produced. Over 15 million were made before production ended in 1927. By 1910, the main features of many later cars had been established: a four-stroke engine mounted at the front, with power being transmitted to the rear wheels via a drive shaft.

Valve

Cylinder

Piston

Connecting rod

INSIDE AN ENGINE
This 1925 Morris engine is a basic power unit for a family car. Its four in-line cylinders have aluminium pistons. The valves are opened by push rods operated by a camshaft and closed by springs. Power is transmitted via the crankshaft to the gearbox. The clutch disconnects the engine from the gearbox when the driver changes gear.

Cinema

In 1824, an English doctor, P.M. Roget, first explained the phenomenon of "persistence of vision". He noticed that if you see an object in a series of closely similar positions in a rapid sequence, your eyes tend to see a single moving object. It did not take people long to realise that a moving image could be created with a series of still images, and within 10 years scientists all over the world were developing a variety of devices for creating this illusion. Most of these machines remained little more than novelties or toys but, combined with improvements in illumination systems for magic lanterns and with developments in photography, they helped the progress of cinema technology. The first sucessful public showing of moving images created by cinematography was in the 1890s by two French brothers, Auguste and Louis Lumière. They created a combined camera and projector, the Cinématographe, which recorded the pictures on a celluloid strip.

ROUND AND ROUND
In the late 1870s, Eadweard Muybridge designed the zoopraxiscope for projecting moving images on a screen. The images were a sequence of pictures based on photographs, painted on a glass disc, which rotated to create a moving picture.

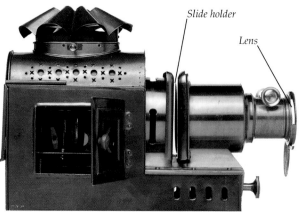

Slide holder

Lens

SILVER SCREEN
The Lumières' system was used for the first regular film shows in Europe. The brothers opened a cinema in a café basement in 1895.

CINÉMATOGRAPHE LUMIÈRE

Lens hood to prevent stray light reaching lens

MAGIC LIGHT-SHOW *above*
In a magic lantern, images on a transparent slide are projected on a screen using a lens and a light source. Early magic lanterns used a candle; later, limelight or carbon arcs were used to give more intense illumination.

An early movie-maker at work

MOVING PICTURES
The Lumières were among the first to demonstrate projected moving images. Their Cinématographe worked like a magic lantern, but projected images from a continuous strip of film.

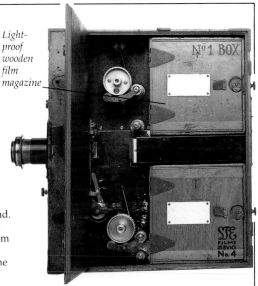

STRIP FEATURES *above*
In the 1880s, Muybridge produced thousands of sequences of photographs that showed animals and people in motion. He placed 12 or more cameras side by side and used electro-magnetic shutters that fired at precise, split-second intervals as the subject moved in front of them.

LONG AND WINDING PATH *right*
Movie film must be wound through the camera and projector at between 16 and 24 frames a second. Many metres of film are needed for shows lasting more than a few minutes. This English camera from 1909 had two 120 m (400 ft) film magazines. Film comes out of the first magazine, passes through the gate, and is fed into the lower magazine.

Light-proof wooden film magazine

GLORIOUS TECHNICOLOR
Colour movies became common in the late 1940s. This Technicolor three-strip camera of 1932 has a prism beamsplitter behind the lens which exposes three separate negative films – sensitive to red, blue, and green. The three images were dyed and then combined to make a single full-colour print film for projecting.

Film spools

Prism beamsplitter

Viewfinder

Film gate

Film housing door - opened to reveal film winding system and film gate

Film revolution counter

Radio

GUGLIELMO MARCONI, experimenting in his parents' attic near Bologna, developed the first radio. Fascinated by the idea of using radio waves to send messages through the air he created an invention that was to change the world, making wireless communication over long distances possible and transforming the entertainment business. As a transmitter he used an electric spark generator invented by Heinrich Hertz. Radio waves from this were detected by a "coherer", the invention of Frenchman Edouard Branly. The coherer turned the radio waves into an electric current. Marconi made an electric bell ring by sending radio signals across the room. That was in 1894. Within eight years, he was sending radio messages 4,800 km (3,000 miles) across the Atlantic.

A BRIGHT SPARK *above*
In 1888 Heinrich Hertz, a German physicist, made an electric spark jump between pairs of metal spheres, creating a current in a circuit nearby. Hertz was studying electromagnetic waves, a type of radiation that includes visible light, radio waves, X-rays, infra-red waves, and ultraviolet light.

Glass bulb

Positive electrode (anode)

Grid

Filament (negative electrode - cathode)

Diode

HEATING UP
Early radio receivers were not sensitive. In 1904, Englishman John Ambrose Fleming first used a diode (a device with two electrodes) as a better detector of radio waves. It was a type of thermionic valve (from the Greek "therm", meaning heat and "ion", the electrically charged particles of atoms). Diodes convert alternating electric currents into direct ones, for use in electric circuits.

Triode

CARRIER WAVES
Thermionic valves developed into the triode of 1906, with a third electrode, the grid, between the cathode and anode. Triodes allow telephone messages and microphone signals to be amplified. The amplified signals are combined with special radio waves known as carrier waves so that they can be transmitted over great distances.

IT'S THE CAT'S WHISKERS
When radio stations first started broadcasting in the early 1920s, listeners tuned in using receivers made up of silicon crystals or lead compounds and thin wires popularly known as cat's whiskers. The radio signals were weak, so headphones were used. They contain a pair of devices that convert varying electric currents into sound waves to reproduce broadcasts.

ACROSS THE AIRWAVES
Marconi developed radio as the first practical system of wireless telegraphy, which made possible uninterrupted communication over land and sea.

Electrical connections to battery

HEAVY SOUNDS
Valves and other radio components needed a direct current supply. Also, until the 1940s, mains electricity was not widespread. Radio sets of the 1930s and 1940s ran off large, powerful batteries. The resulting radio receiver was big and heavy. A separate loudspeaker was used with this model.

Tuning condenser

Coils

Valve

Crystal

Cat's whisker

Tuning dials

Volume control

WHAT THE WHISKER DID
The crystal detector only worked when the cat's whisker made a point contact with the crystal. It was often a problem establishing the contact, so crystal sets were difficult to use. They were soon superseded by sets using thermionic valves.

WORDS AND PICTURES
In the 1920s, valves like this triode were important not only in allowing the first speech broadcast from England to Australia – by Marconi in 1924 – but also in the development of television cameras, transmitters, and receivers.

GOOD RECEPTION
This early valve receiver had a loudspeaker built into the cabinet.

Plug-in base

RADIO COMES TO EVERY HOME
By the 1920s, many radio transmitters had been built and radio was within reach of many households in Europe and the USA.

GATHER ROUND
This detail from a painting by W. R. Scott shows people gathering round a radio receiver at a Christmas party. In 1922, when this picture was painted, radio was still a new attraction for most people.

Inventions in the home

Scientist Michael Faraday (1791-1867) discovered how to generate electricity in 1831. But it was many years before electricity was used around the home. At first, large houses and factories installed their own generators and used electricity for lighting. The electric filament lamp was demonstrated in 1879. In 1882, the first large electricity power station was built in New York. Gradually, as people began to realise how appliances could save work in the home, mechanical items, such as early vacuum cleaners, were replaced by more efficient electrical versions. As the middle classes came to rely less and less on domestic servants, labour-saving appliances became more popular. Electric motors were applied to food mixers and hairdriers around 1920. Electric kettles, cookers, and heaters, making use of the heating effect of an electric current, had also appeared by this time. Some of these items were very similar in design to those used today.

WATER CLOSET
The first description of a flush toilet or water closet was published by Sir John Harrington in 1591. But the idea did not catch on widely until mains drainage was installed in major cities. London's main drainage, for example, was not in operation until the 1860s. By this time several improved versions of the W.C. had been patented.

KEEPING COOL
Electric refrigerators began to appear in the 1920s. They revolutionized food storage.

TEA'S UP
In the automatic tea-maker of 1902, levers, springs, and the steam from the kettle activate stages in the teamaking process. A bell is struck to tell you that the tea is ready.

ON THE BOIL
The Swan electric kettle of 1921 was the first with a totally immersed heating element. Earlier models had elements in a separate compartment in the bottom of the kettle, which wasted a lot of heat.

THE "WILSON" COOKER is Perfection for Baking Bread Pastry and Tea Cakes

COOK'S FRIEND
Before the 19th century, you had to light a fire to cook food. By 1879, an electric cooker had been designed in which food was heated by electricity passing through insulated wire wound round the cooking pot. In the 1890s, heating elements were made as iron plates with wires beneath. The modern element, which can be bent to any shape, came into use in the 1920s.

Heating element

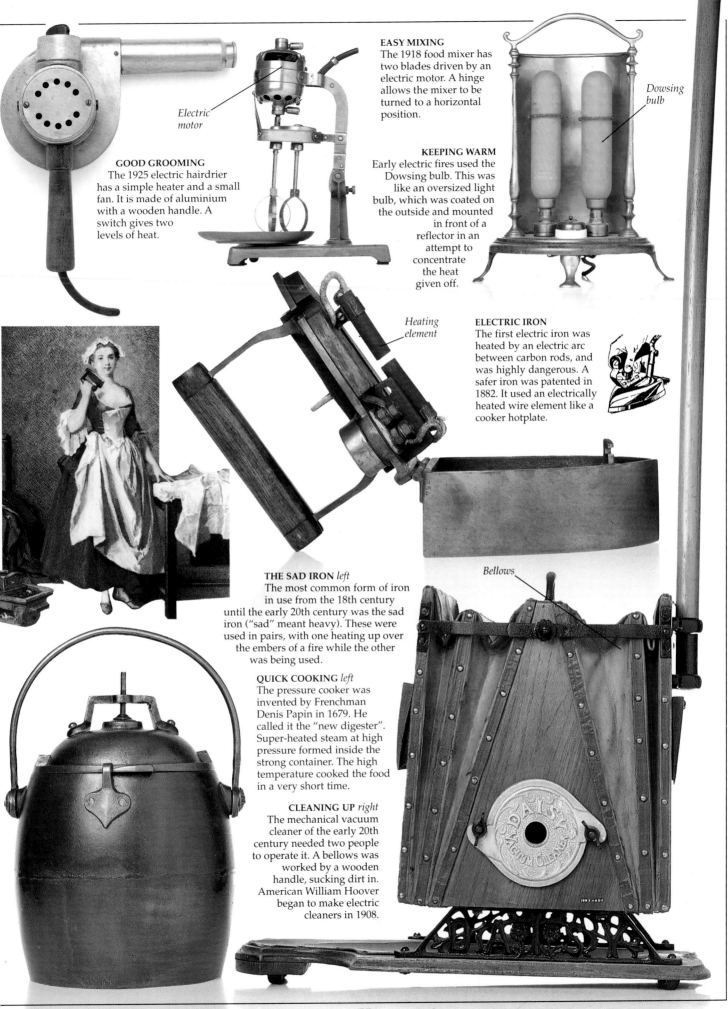

EASY MIXING
The 1918 food mixer has two blades driven by an electric motor. A hinge allows the mixer to be turned to a horizontal position.

Electric motor

Dowsing bulb

GOOD GROOMING
The 1925 electric hairdrier has a simple heater and a small fan. It is made of aluminium with a wooden handle. A switch gives two levels of heat.

KEEPING WARM
Early electric fires used the Dowsing bulb. This was like an oversized light bulb, which was coated on the outside and mounted in front of a reflector in an attempt to concentrate the heat given off.

Heating element

ELECTRIC IRON
The first electric iron was heated by an electric arc between carbon rods, and was highly dangerous. A safer iron was patented in 1882. It used an electrically heated wire element like a cooker hotplate.

Bellows

THE SAD IRON *left*
The most common form of iron in use from the 18th century until the early 20th century was the sad iron ("sad" meant heavy). These were used in pairs, with one heating up over the embers of a fire while the other was being used.

QUICK COOKING *left*
The pressure cooker was invented by Frenchman Denis Papin in 1679. He called it the "new digester". Super-heated steam at high pressure formed inside the strong container. The high temperature cooked the food in a very short time.

CLEANING UP *right*
The mechanical vacuum cleaner of the early 20th century needed two people to operate it. A bellows was worked by a wooden handle, sucking dirt in. American William Hoover began to make electric cleaners in 1908.

The cathode ray tube

IN 1887, PHYSICIST William Crookes was investigating the properties of electricity. He used a glass tube containing two metal plates, the electrodes. When a high voltage was applied and the air pumped out of the tube, electricity passed between the electrodes and caused a glow in the tube. As the pressure fell (approaching a vacuum) the light went out, yet the glass itself glowed. Crookes called the rays which caused this Cathode Rays; they were, in fact, an invisible flow of electrons. Later Ferdinand Braun created a tube with an end wall coated with a substance that glowed when struck by cathode rays. This was the forerunner of the modern TV receiver tube.

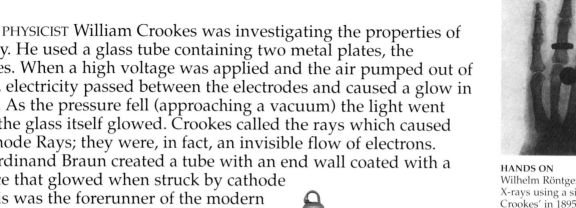

HANDS ON
Wilhelm Röntgen discovered X-rays using a similar tube to Crookes' in 1895.

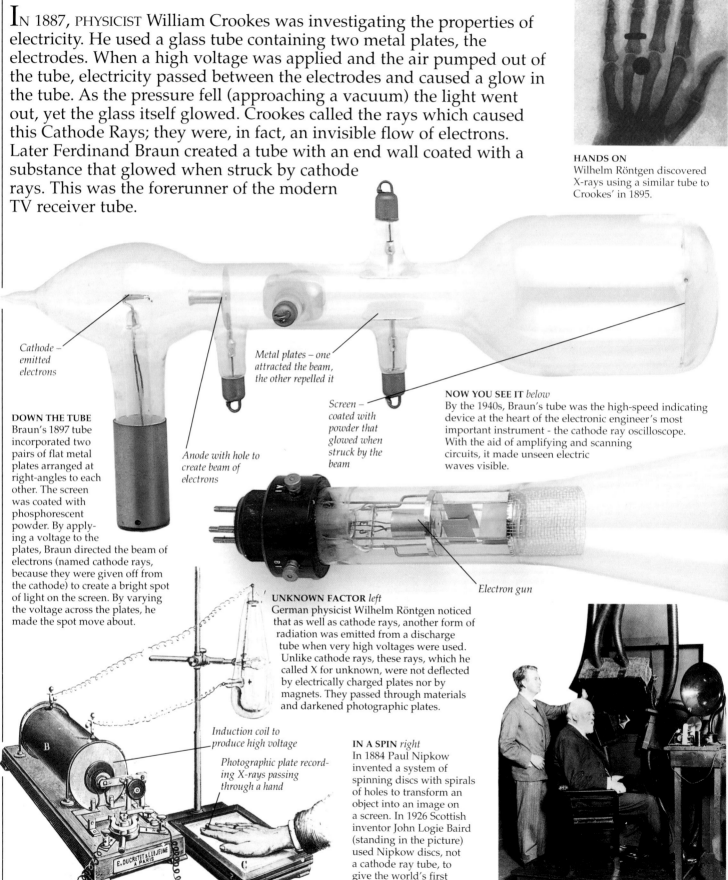

Cathode – emitted electrons

Metal plates – one attracted the beam, the other repelled it

Anode with hole to create beam of electrons

Screen – coated with powder that glowed when struck by the beam

DOWN THE TUBE
Braun's 1897 tube incorporated two pairs of flat metal plates arranged at right-angles to each other. The screen was coated with phosphorescent powder. By applying a voltage to the plates, Braun directed the beam of electrons (named cathode rays, because they were given off from the cathode) to create a bright spot of light on the screen. By varying the voltage across the plates, he made the spot move about.

NOW YOU SEE IT *below*
By the 1940s, Braun's tube was the high-speed indicating device at the heart of the electronic engineer's most important instrument - the cathode ray oscilloscope. With the aid of amplifying and scanning circuits, it made unseen electric waves visible.

Electron gun

UNKNOWN FACTOR *left*
German physicist Wilhelm Röntgen noticed that as well as cathode rays, another form of radiation was emitted from a discharge tube when very high voltages were used. Unlike cathode rays, these rays, which he called X for unknown, were not deflected by electrically charged plates nor by magnets. They passed through materials and darkened photographic plates.

Induction coil to produce high voltage

Photographic plate recording X-rays passing through a hand

IN A SPIN *right*
In 1884 Paul Nipkow invented a system of spinning discs with spirals of holes to transform an object into an image on a screen. In 1926 Scottish inventor John Logie Baird (standing in the picture) used Nipkow discs, not a cathode ray tube, to give the world's first demonstration of television.

Single-beam gun

Electromagnetic coil to direct electron beams

CHEAPER TV
In the late 1960s, the Japanese firm Sony developed and patented the Trinitron system, a cathode ray tube with a different design from RCA's original colour tube. This meant that they did not have to pay fees to RCA for every tube they made.

Electron gun producing 3 separate beams

Trinitron tube

TELEVISION GOES PUBLIC
In 1936 the BBC started the first public high-definition television service from this studio at Alexandra Palace, London. At first they used both Baird's system and one using the cathode ray tube. The latter gave the best results and Baird's system was never used again. In 1939 RCA started America's first fully electronic television service.

FASTER THAN THE EYE CAN NOTICE *below*
Until the 1960s, most home television receivers produced black and white pictures and operated with valves (p. 52). The "tube" consisted of a single electron gun producing a beam that was made to scan the screen up to 50 times a second. As techniques improved, the length of the tube was shortened.

Phosphor screen

IN FRONT OF THE BOX *above*
Early television sets, such as this RCA Victor model, had small screens but contained such a mass of additional components that they were housed in large boxes. At the time, many such sets cost as much as a small car.

Electron gun

Flight

THE FIRST CREATURES to fly in a humanmade craft were a cockerel, a duck, and a sheep. They were sent up in a hot-air balloon made by the French Montgolfier brothers in September 1783. When the animals landed safely, the brothers were encouraged to send two of their friends, Pilâtre de Rozier and the Marquis d'Arlandes, on a 25-minute flight over Paris. Among the earliest pioneers of powered flight were Englishmen William Henson and John Stringfellow, who built a model aircraft powered by a steam engine in the 1840s. We do not know whether it flew or not – it may well have failed because of the heavy weight and low power of the engine. But it did have many of the features of the successful aeroplane. It was the American Wright brothers who first achieved powered, controlled flight in a full-size aeroplane. Their *Flyer* of 1903 was powered by a lightweight petrol engine.

AIRBORNE CARRIAGE
Henson and Stringfellow's "Aerial steam carriage" had many features that were taken up by later aircraft designers. It had a separate tail with rudders and elevators, and upward-sloping wings. The craft looks strange but it was a surprisingly practical design.

Wooden and canvas wing

MECHANICAL WING
Some 500 years ago, Leonardo da Vinci designed a number of flying machines. These mostly had mechanical flapping wings. They were bound to fail because of the great effort needed to flap the wings. Leonardo also designed a simple helicopter.

FIRST FLIGHT *below*
On 4 June, 1783, Joseph and Etienne Montgolfier demonstrated a paper hot-air balloon. It climbed to about 1,000 m (3,300 ft). Later in the same year, the brothers sent up their animal and human passengers.

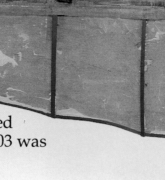

GLIDING FREE *above*
The first piloted glider was built by German engineer Otto Lilienthal. He made many flights between 1891 and 1896, when he was killed as his glider crashed. His work showed the basics of controlling a craft in the air.

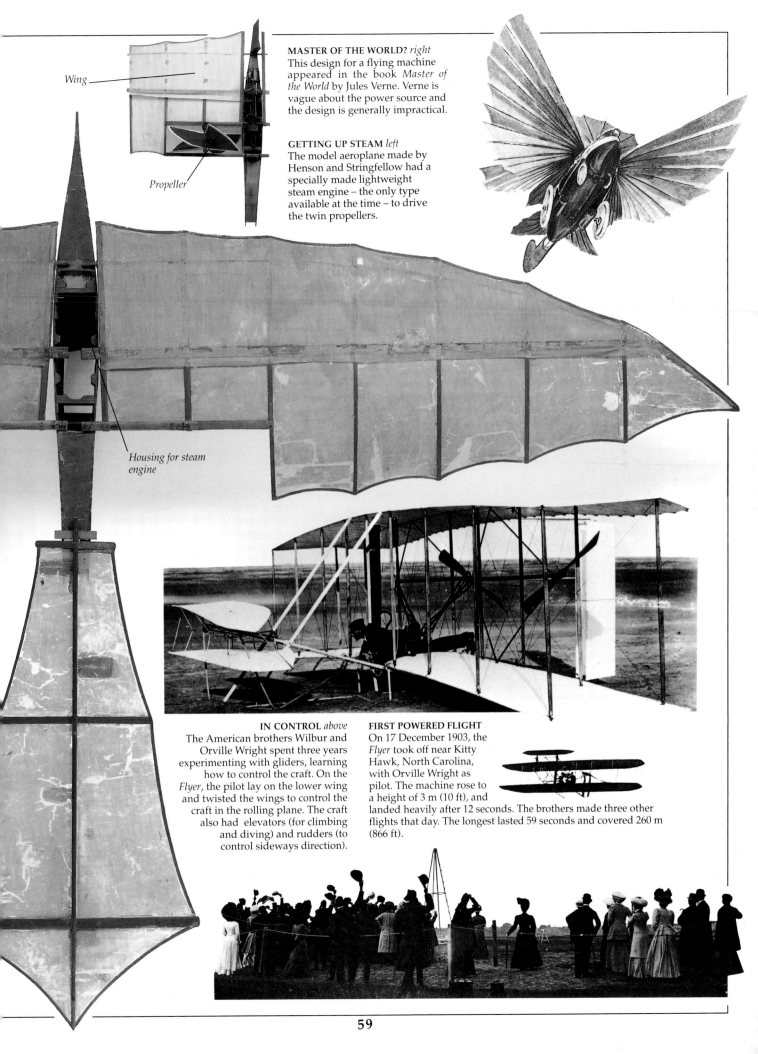

MASTER OF THE WORLD? *right*
This design for a flying machine appeared in the book *Master of the World* by Jules Verne. Verne is vague about the power source and the design is generally impractical.

GETTING UP STEAM *left*
The model aeroplane made by Henson and Stringfellow had a specially made lightweight steam engine – the only type available at the time – to drive the twin propellers.

Wing

Propeller

Housing for steam engine

IN CONTROL *above*
The American brothers Wilbur and Orville Wright spent three years experimenting with gliders, learning how to control the craft. On the *Flyer*, the pilot lay on the lower wing and twisted the wings to control the craft in the rolling plane. The craft also had elevators (for climbing and diving) and rudders (to control sideways direction).

FIRST POWERED FLIGHT
On 17 December 1903, the *Flyer* took off near Kitty Hawk, North Carolina, with Orville Wright as pilot. The machine rose to a height of 3 m (10 ft), and landed heavily after 12 seconds. The brothers made three other flights that day. The longest lasted 59 seconds and covered 260 m (866 ft).

Plastics

Plastics are materials which can easily be formed into different shapes. They were first used to make imitations of other materials, but it soon became clear that they had useful properties of their own. They are made up of long, chain-like molecules formed by a process (called polymerization) that joins small molecules together. The resulting long molecules give plastics their special properties. The first plastic, Parkesine, was made by modifying cellulose, a chainlike molecule found in most plants. The first truly synthetic plastic was Bakelite, which was invented in 1907. The chemists of the 1920s and 1930s developed ways of making plastics from substances found in oil. Their efforts resulted in a range of materials with different heat, electrical, optical, and moulding properties. Plastics such as polyethylene, nylon, and acrylics, are widely used today.

IMITATION IVORY
Early plastics often had the appearance and feel of ivory, and carried names such as Ivoride. Materials like this were used for knife handles and combs.

Moulded decoration

IN FLAMES
In the 1860s, a plastic called Celluloid was developed. It was used as a substitute for ivory to make billiard balls, and for small items like this powder box. The new material made little impact at first but, in 1889, George Eastman began using it as a base for photographic film. Unfortunately, it had the disadvantage that it easily caught fire and sometimes exploded.

THE FIRST PLASTIC *right*
In 1862 Alexander Parkes made a hard material that could be moulded into shapes. Called "Parkesine", it was the first semi-synthetic plastic.

Hard, smooth surface

HEAT-PROOF
Leo Baekeland, a Belgium-born chemist working in America, made a plastic from chemicals found in coal tar. His plastic, which he called Bakelite, was different from earlier plastics because heat made it set hard instead of causing it to melt.

Celluloid box

AROUND THE HOUSE
Plastics of the 1920s and 30s, like urea formaldehyde, were tough, non-toxic, and could be made any colour with synthetic pigments. They were used for boxes, clock cases, piano keys and lamps.

Heat-proof Bakelite container

Marble-effect surface

Acrylic glasses

Film

Imitation sponge

Expanded
polystyrene
egg
box

Nylon thread

PLASTIC FOAM *above*
Polystyrene was first made in the 1920s. It
comes in two forms: a hard form and a
lightweight foam full of small holes called
expanded poly-
styrene.

Buttons
and pen

Toy bricks

NYLON ROPE
Nylon provides
great strength in a
narrow thickness,
making it ideal for
rope.

Moulded
polyethylene
spade and
racket

*Separate
nylon fibres*

SHAPES AND SIZES
Plastic can be formed into
intricate shapes, like this
fine netting.

PLASTIC FIBRES *left*
It was American chemist Wallace Carothers who
produced a plastic called nylon in 1934. It was like
artificial silk and could be drawn out into thin threads
and woven into cloth or twined round to create rope as
strong as steel cable. Polyester, another plastic suitable
for fibres, was discovered in 1941. Polyester fibres are
woven into cloth for shirts, trousers, and dresses.

Plastic spanner

Polyethylene
flower

The silicon chip

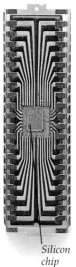

EARLY RADIOS AND TELEVISION SETS used valves (p. 52) to manipulate their electric currents. These were large, had a short life, and were costly to produce. In 1947, scientists at the Bell Telephone Laboratories in the United States invented the smaller, cheaper, and more reliable transistor to do the same job. With the development of spacecraft, still smaller components were needed, and by the end of the 1960s, thousands of transistors and other electronic components were being crammed on to chips of silicon only 5 mm square. These chips were soon being used in many other areas, replacing the mechanical control devices in items ranging from dishwashers to cameras. They were also taking the place of the bulky electronic circuits in computers. A computer that took a whole room to house could be contained in a case that would fit on top of a desk. A revolution in information technology followed, with computers being used for everything from playing games to administering government departments.

BABBAGE'S ENGINE
The ancestor of the computer was Charles Babbage's "Difference Engine", a mechanical calculating device. Today tiny chips do the job of such cumbersome mechanisms.

Silicon wafer containing several hundred tiny chips

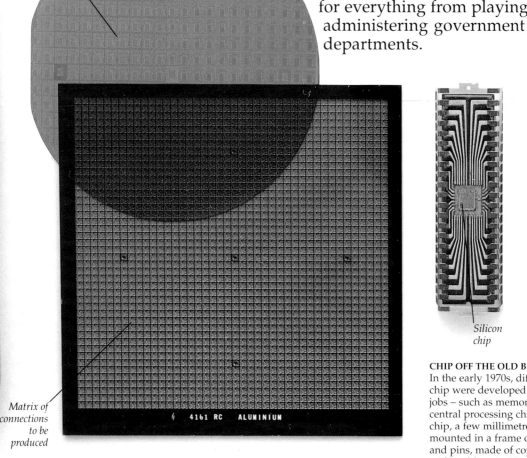

Matrix of connections to be produced

SILICON CRYSTAL
Silicon is usually found combined with oxygen as silica, one form of which is quartz. Pure silicon is dark grey, hard, non-metallic, and forms crystals.

4161 RC ALUMINIUM

MAKING A CHIP
The electrical components and connections are built up in layers on a wafer of pure silicon 0.5 mm thick. First, chemical impurities are embedded in specific regions of the silicon to alter their electrical properties. Then aluminium connections (the equivalent of conventional wires) are laid on top.

Silicon chip

Ceramic housing

CHIP OFF THE OLD BLOCK
In the early 1970s, different types of chip were developed to do specific jobs – such as memory chips and central processing chips. Each silicon chip, a few millimetres square, is mounted in a frame of connections and pins, made of copper coated with gold or tin. Fine gold wires link connector pads around the edge of the chip to the frame. The whole assembly is housed in a protective insulating block.

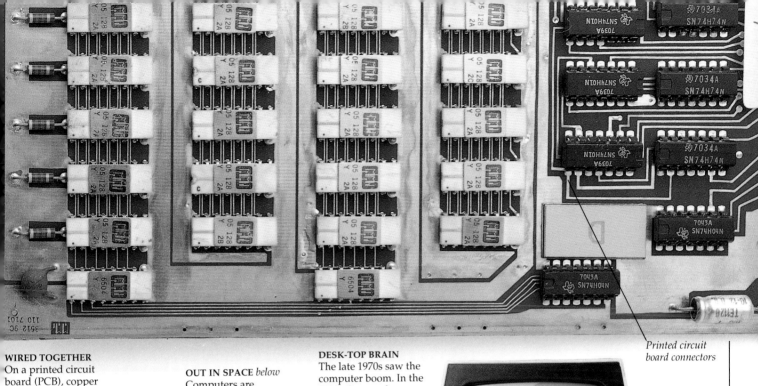

Printed circuit board connectors

WIRED TOGETHER
On a printed circuit board (PCB), copper surrounding the tracks on an insulating board is etched away. Components, including silicon chips, are plugged or soldered into holes in the PCB.

OUT IN SPACE *below*
Computers are essential for spacecraft like this satellite. The silicon chip means that control devices can be housed in the limited space on board.

DESK-TOP BRAIN
The late 1970s saw the computer boom. In the USA, Commodore introduced the PET, one of the first mass-produced personal computers. It was used mainly in businesses and schools.

Visual display unit (VDU)

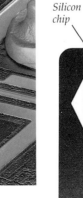

Keyboard

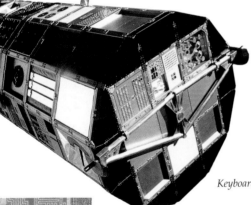

ON THE RIGHT TRACK
Under a microscope, the circuitry of a chip looks like a network of aluminium tracks and islands of silicon, treated to conduct electricity.

MAKING CONNECTIONS
A close-up shows the connector wires attached to the silicon. Robots have to be used to join the wires to the chip since the components are so tiny and must be very accurately positioned.

SMART PHONE CARD
Smart cards contain a microprocessor and memory on a single silicon chip. When this card is inserted into a phone, the chip receives power and data through the gold contacts. It can then do security checks and record how many units have been used.

Silicon chip

TELECARTE
50 UNITES

Did you know?

AMAZING FACTS

TetraPak milk carton

The TetraPak carton was launched in 1952 by Swedish businessman, Ruben Rausing. Its clever design is ideal for holding liquids such as milk, juice, and soup.

Bar codes were first introduced in 1974. A laser scanner "reads" the bar-coded number so that a computer can look up information such as name and price.

Modern snowmobile

The first hovercraft, SR.N1, was launched in 1959. It was designed by a British engineer, Christopher Cockerell. The craft glided across water or land, supported on a cushion of air that was contained by a rubberized skirt.

The first ever computer game was Space War. It was developed in 1962 by a college student at the Massachusetts Institute of Technology (MIT).

In 2001, Robert Tools was fitted with the first self-contained artificial heart. The grapefruit-sized AbioCor runs on a battery fitted in the ribcage. Earlier artificial hearts needed an outside power source, so anyone who received one had wires sticking out of his or her chest.

The Chinese invented the first toothbrushes about 500 years ago. They were made from pigs' bristles. The first nylon brushes were made in the 1930s.

The poma® wearable computer

Wearable computers for the consumer market were unveiled in 2002, when American company Xybernaut® showed off poma® to the world. "Poma®" is short for "portable multimedia appliance". The central processing unit clips on to the user's belt, while a 2.5 cm (1 in) square monitor sits in front of one eye.

Global positioning system (GPS) receivers were developed for the U.S. Air Force in the 1970s. By cross-referencing information from several satellites, a receiver can work out its precise location.

The Aqua-Lung was invented by French oceanographer, Jacques Cousteau, who also developed an improved method of filming underwater. Cousteau used his inventions to show television viewers the wonders of the undersea world.

Diver and inventor Jacques Cousteau

The modern snowmobile was created in the 1950s by Canadian inventor Joseph-Armand Bombardier. Rather like a motorbike on skis, it is used in snowy regions by foresters, rescue workers, and the police. It is also popular as a leisure and racing vehicle.

Some of the equipment that John Logie Baird used to build his first television system included a bicycle light and a knitting needle!

The computer mouse was invented in 1965 by Doug Engelbart. It was not called a mouse, though. He called it an "x-y position indicator".

The first compact discs (CDs) went on sale in 1982. They were a joint invention by two electronics companies, Philips and Sony. At first, the CD was used to store only sounds. Today it also carries written words, pictures, and even movies.

An ancient Greek designed the world's first vending machine. Around A.D. 60, Hero of Alexandria came up with a drinks dispenser. Putting a coin in the slot moved a cork stopper, to make a drink of water trickle out.

Teflon, the non-stick plastic pan coating, was found by accident. Chemist Roy Plunkett discovered it in 1938, while testing the gas tetrafluoroethylene. Teflon is able to withstand temperatures as low as −270 °C (−450 °F) and as high as 250 °C (480 °F).

Bubble gum was invented in 1928 by Walter Diemer. He adapted an existing recipe for chewing gum so that it could be used to blow bubbles.

QUESTIONS AND ANSWERS

Dean Kamen on his Segway HT

Q Are there any famous contemporary inventors?

A It seems as if the past is full of famous inventors but, in the modern world, products are usually created by teams of people working for large companies. Dean Kamen is one of the few famous names in the world of inventing. While still a student, Kamen designed a wearable infusion pump that injects sick patients with exact doses of the drugs they need. Next he developed portable insulin pumps and kidney dialysis machines. Not all of Kamen's innovations are in the medical field. In 2001 he unveiled his Segway Human Transporter (HT), a self-balancing transportation device with an integral gyroscope. Kamen envisages that the Segway HT will revolutionize short-distance travel, particularly in cities. Postal workers, for example, will be able to make deliveries far more quickly and efficiently.

Q Which invention shrank the world in three decades?

A The internet began life in 1963 in the United States as the ARPAnet, a network of computers linked up to protect military data in the event of a nuclear attack. Under ARPAnet there were key advances: e-mail (1971); telnet, a way to control a computer from a distance (1972); and file transfer protocol (FTP), which helps transfer files (1973). By the 1980s the internet had developed into an international network. But it took until the mid-1990s for world wide web (WWW) technology to improve enough to make the internet a vital tool in universities, businesses, and homes. The web allows people to swap text, sound, still pictures, and movies around the world – in a matter of seconds.

Q Why are most inventions created by companies rather than individuals?

A The Japanese electronics company Sony is famous for its ground-breaking inventions including the Walkman, PlayStation, and AIBO robot dog. Few people could name any of the individuals involved in the creation of these products. That is because, as technology becomes more complex, whole teams of specialists are needed to work on different aspects of the invention. Also, building and testing new technologies requires sophisticated, costly machinery that only large corporations can afford. Such companies market new inventions under their own name, a brand that customers will recognize. Even if the product had been invented by an individual employee, the company probably would not market it under the inventor's name. For one thing, at some point in the future, the inventor may go to work for a rival firm.

Sony's robot dog, AIBO

Q How do inventors safeguard their best ideas?

A The only way to be sure that no-one steals the design of a new invention is to patent it. Each country has its own patent office, where officials register plans, drawings, and specifications. Only an invention that is truly new can be patented. After that, the inventor can sue anyone who tries to make or sell products based on the same idea, unless they have paid for permission to use it.

Q Could inventions ever outwit inventors?

A At this moment, several scientists are working to build computers with artificial intelligence. These would be capable of testing ideas through trial and error, thereby learning from their mistakes. In 2002 the most advanced machines possessed the mental capacity of a beetle, but designs are always improving.

Record Breakers

⌛ **FASTEST LAND VEHICLE**
A jet-powered car called *Thrust 2* set the one mile land speed record in Nevada in 1983. It ran at 1,019.47 km/h (633.47 mph). The car was designed by British engineer, John Ackroyd.

⌛ **FASTEST TRANSISTOR**
A silicon transistor that switches on and off 1.5 trillion times a second is due for use in computers from 2007. Some of the Intel transistor's components are just 20 nanometres long – that is 1/4,000 the width of a human hair.

⌛ **MOST PATENTS**
American inventor Thomas Edison filed 1,093 patents during his lifetime. They included 141 patents for batteries, and 389 for electric light and power.

⌛ **BIGGEST RADIO TELESCOPE**
The biggest single-dish radio telescope is 305 m (1,000 ft) across. However, the Very Large Array (VLA) in New Mexico is even more powerful. It is made up of 27 dishes, working together as a single telescope.

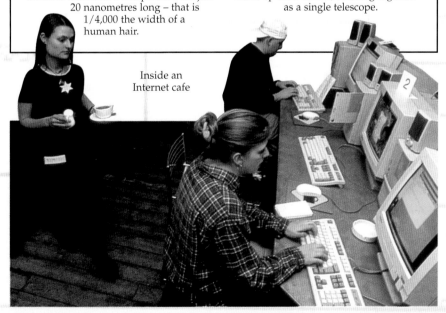

Inside an Internet cafe

Timeline of inventions

Deer antler pick axe

Silicon wafer, 1981

THE HISTORY OF INVENTION begins when our earliest ancestors started to use tools, more than three million years ago. Since then, humankind has continued to employ intelligence and resourcefulness to make useful technologies that help change our world. Any timeline of invention must miss out far more than it includes. Here are just a few important tools, instruments, and machines that have been invented over the last 10,000 years.

• 8000 B.C.
FLINT MINING
Prehistoric miners dug deep shafts in search of flints – hard stones that could be shaped into useful, sharp tools. As flints were mostly embedded in soft chalk, the miners used deer antlers as simple picks.

8000 B.C.

• 400 B.C.
CROSSBOW
The ancient Greeks came up with the first crossbow, which they called the gastrophetes. A crossbow can fire an arrow much further than an ordinary bow.

Crossbow

400 B.C.

• 100 B.C.
SCREW PRESS
The screw press was invented by the Greeks. They would place grapes, olives, or even clothes between the two boards. They turned the screw to press the top board down hard, squeezing out the juice, oil, or excess water.

Screw press

100 B.C.

• A.D. 550
ASTROLABE
The astrolabe was an instrument that enabled travellers to find their latitude by studying the position of the stars. It was first invented by Arab astronomers.

Astrolabe

A.D. 550

Leclanché cell

• AD 1866
LECLANCHÉ CELL
French engineer Georges Leclanché created the forerunner of the modern battery. The negative terminal was a jar with a zinc rod in an ammonium chloride solution. Inside this was the positive terminal, a smaller pot with a carbon rod in manganese dioxide.

A.D. 1866

• A.D. 1892
VISCOSE RAYON
This artificial fibre was the first realistic alternative to silk. Three British chemists discovered the process for making it, starting out with a natural ingredient, cellulose, found in cotton and wood pulp.

Rayon fabric

A.D. 1892

• A.D. 1902
TEA-MAKING ALARM CLOCK
Frank Clarke's automatic tea-maker was a dangerous device. It ignited methylated spirits, which boiled water in the copper kettle. The kettle tipped to fill a teapot – and sounded the alarm.

Automatic tea maker

A.D. 1902

Roman scales

• 4000 B.C.
SCALES
The Sumerians invented the beam balance, where a measuring pan is hung from either end of a wooden or metal beam. Later peoples, including the Romans, improved on this basic principle.

4000 B.C.

Chinese writing

• 1500 B.C.
CHINESE WRITING
Chinese is the oldest surviving written language. Like the first written language, Sumerian cuneiform, Chinese characters started out as pictograms – pictures of objects and ideas – which were gradually stylized.

1500 B.C.

• 600 B.C.
ARCHIMEDEAN SCREW
This device is named after the Greek thinker Archimedes, who described one he saw being used in Egypt around 260 B.C. The screw is a pump. It pushes water up along the "thread" of the cylinder as the user turns the screw.

Archimedean screw

600 B.C.

• A.D. 1088
MECHANICAL CLOCK
The first mechanical clock was a complicated tower of wheels and gears, invented by Su Sung. It used a waterwheel that moved the mechanism forward every time one of its buckets filled up. Every 24 hours, a metal globe representing the Earth turned on its axis once.

Su Sung's mechanical clock tower

A.D. 1088

• A.D. 1643
BAROMETER
The barometer, an instrument that measures air pressure, was invented by Italian physicist, Evangelista Torricelli. He put a dish over the end of a closed tube of mercury, then inverted both of them. The mercury fell until its level balanced the pressure of the air.

Torricelli's barometer

A.D. 1643

• A.D. 1788
THRESHING MACHINE
Threshing means separating grains of corn from the husk, or chaff. It used to be done by beating harvested corn with a stick, but in 1788 Scottish millwright Andrew Meickle invented a machine to do the job.

Threshing machine

A.D. 1788

• A.D. 1948
POLAROID CAMERA
The first "instant" camera was the Polaroid Land camera, invented by American Edwin Land. The camera used special film, which contained the necessary developing chemicals. One minute after taking the picture, a brown and white photograph came out.

Modern Polaroid camera

A.D. 1948

• A.D. 1965
COMPUTER MOUSE
The mouse was invented by U.S. engineer Doug Engelbart in 1965. The first personal computer to use it was the Apple Mac, launched in 1984. Until then, people had to use keyboard commands.

COMPUTER MOUSE

A.D. 1965

• A.D. 1983
DYSON CYCLONIC CLEANER
British inventor James Dyson came up with the first bagless vacuum cleaner. His inspiration was an industrial cyclone, a whirling device used by factories to suck dust particles from air. Dyson made his first model of a bagless cleaner in 1978. His G-Force cyclonic cleaner went on sale in Japan eight years later.

Dyson multi-cyclone cleaner

A.D. 1983

Find out more

The food mixer is just one of many inventions in the home

IF YOU ARE ALL FIRED UP about inventions, you will soon notice that you come across hundreds of them every day – and many of them are in your own home. Visits to museums can give lots of helpful information about inventions, or hands-on demonstrations of how they work. Look out for useful books, websites, and television programmes, too. Best of all, see if you can come up with some inventions of your own. Start with sketches and descriptions, then build up to making a working model. Good luck!

OLD VALVE RADIO
All inventors learn valuable lessons by looking at the inventions of the past. Look out in junk shops for cheap old radios or other machines. Compare your finds to their modern versions. How have radios changed since this one was made? What features have disappeared? Which are still there? And what can modern radios do that this one cannot?

USEFUL WEBSITES

- A website with a timeline, plus A-Zs of inventors and inventions
  www.inventors.about.com
- Lots of explanations of scientific principles and inventions
  www.howstuffworks.com
- A Smithsonian website dedicated to the lives of inventors
  www.si.edu/lemelson/centerpieces/ilives/index.html
- Website for the Tech Museum of Innovation, California
  www.thetech.org

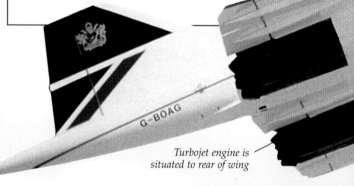

Turbojet engine is situated to rear of wing

CONCORDE, AN INVENTION OF THE SKIES
Fly away on holiday, or simply look up, to see some of humankind's most amazing inventions – aircraft. Jet passenger planes have been around since 1952, while the first supersonic craft, *Concorde*, made its maiden flight in 1969. Although only 14 of the planes entered service, it is still possible to see them flying today. Flying at twice the speed of sound, *Concorde* cut the time of a transatlantic flight to three hours 50 minutes.

GEODESIC DOME
This eyecatching building is La Géode, an OMNIMAX cinema where visitors can enjoy the latest cinematic technologies, including a 360° movie screen. It is in the Parc de la Villette, Paris. If you cannot get to Paris, see if there is an OMNIMAX or IMAX cinema near you. The quality of the picture and sound is quite an experience.

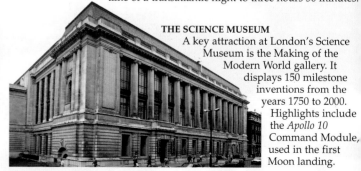

THE SCIENCE MUSEUM
A key attraction at London's Science Museum is the Making of the Modern World gallery. It displays 150 milestone inventions from the years 1750 to 2000. Highlights include the *Apollo 10* Command Module, used in the first Moon landing.

SMART WASHING MACHINE
Familiar appliances are being improved all the time. The latest "smart" kitchen machines are internet linked, so that owners can control them remotely by email. This washing machine will even call out a service engineer if it breaks down.

Rotating drum spins washing

CAMERA CURIOUS
Find out more about a key invention, like the camera. Perhaps you have access to a digital one, or you can read up on the new technology in specialist photography magazines. Digital cameras do not use film. Instead, they have a sensor that converts light (photons) into electical charges (electrons).

Optical viewfinder

YASHICA
Digital Imaging

Places to visit

THE BIG IDEA INVENTOR CENTRE, IRVINE, SCOTLAND, UK
A hands-on exhibition dedicated to the process of inventing.

MUSEUM OF THE HISTORY OF SCIENCE, FLORENCE, ITALY
A collection centred around Rennaissance inventors, including Leonardo da Vinci, Galileo, and Torricelli.

MUSEUM OF SCIENCE AND INDUSTRY, MANCHESTER, UK
Exhibits of steam locomotives, aircraft, and early farm machinery.

PARC DE LA VILLETTE, PARIS, FRANCE
An urban park devoted to science and music, including Cité des Sciences – a huge science museum – and an OMNIMAX cinema.

THE SCIENCE MUSEUM, LONDON, UK
A collection of more than 300,000 objects, charting the progress of invention since the 1700s.

Distinctive, pointy nose cuts through the air

BRITISH AIRWAYS

Wings form streamlined "V" shape

Passengers safe in pressurized cabin

ROBOT WARS
The TV series *Robot Wars* is now popular in over 25 countries. Its enthusiastic contestants call themselves roboteers, but they are also amateur inventors. Anyone can try to compete, so long as they can build a warrior robot with the right specifications – and unique means of attack and defence, of course. Tune in or, better still, set up your own roboteering team.

Glossary

Giant pulleys in a lift

AMPUTATION A type of surgery in which a limb, such as the leg, is removed. It is less common now that medical innovations have made it possible to cure many infections and injuries.

Flint (used as a simple axe)

ANAESTHETIC A substance used to block pain signals from the body to the brain. In medical operations, the anaesthetic effect may be local to the part of the body being operated on, or general, affecting the whole body.

ANGLE Two straight lines leaving a single point make a corner, which can be described by its angle – the portion they would make of any circle centred on the point. Circles are given 360°, so the two hands of a clock at 3pm, which take a quarter of the circle, form an angle of 90°.

ANODE A positive electrode, taken to be the source of current flowing into its surroundings. (see also **ELECTRODE**)

AUTOMATIC Any system or machine that works by itself, without external control or effort by a person.

BEAM In machines and buildings, a strong horizontal supporting bar, made of wood or metal, that carries forces across distances.

CALCULATE In mathematics, to work out the answer according to a rule-governed method. The word comes from the pebbles used in the Roman era to help with maths problems, which were called calx.

CATHODE A negative electrode, which receives current from its surroundings. The flow of electricity into a cathode can be used to coat an object in silver – the object is wired up as a cathode, and attracts tiny particles of silver. (see also **ELECTRODE**)

COMPOUND A chemical substance formed when two or more other substances combine with each other.

CULTIVATE To work towards the best possible growth of plants, especially by ploughing, fertilizing, and weeding fields, and by rotating crops to maintain the balance of nutrients in the soil.

CYLINDER In engines, the tubular chamber in which the pressure is created to push the other parts. In petrol engines, the larger the cylinder (measured in litres), the more power the engine can create.

DIAPHRAGM A thin, strong sheet of material, often circular, designed to flex in the middle. A large diaphragm divides the human body between the chest and the stomach, to aid breathing.

EFFICIENT Describes a machine or system that does a job with very little wasted energy or human effort.

ELECTRICAL Describes any thing or event in which electricity has a significant role.

ELECTRICITY Energy associated with electrically charged particles, usually electrons, either when they are moving, as in a wire, or stationary, as in a battery.

ELECTRODE The source or destination of an electric current in a cell such as a battery. Electrodes can be made from a range of materials, often metallic.

EXPERIMENT A controlled test of a theory, or part of a theory, used to provide evidence for or against a scientific idea.

FLINT A common type of stone, with the useful property of breaking and chipping in a way that produces sharp edges. Flint was widely mined in prehistoric times and used to make simple tools.

FOCUS The point where rays of light meet after passing through a lens.

FORCE A push or pull that can make something move, prevent its moving, or change its motion.

FRICTION The resistance to movement between two surfaces in contact. This force can generate heat, as when rubbing your hands together for warmth.

GEAR A wheel with teeth, which carries power from one moving part to another. On a bicycle, gears are used to allow efficient cycling at different speeds. Closely related to gears are pulleys, which have no teeth and are used with ropes. They are used in lifts and by builders lifting heavy loads.

Chopsticks use a system of leverage

GENERATOR A machine using the motion of a wire coil past magnets to turn movement into electricity – the opposite of an electric motor. A bicycle dynamo is a simple example.

INDUSTRIAL REVOLUTION The dramatic change from a farming society to a mechanized society, first identified in the UK towards the end of the 1700s. Important parts of the process include the relocation of large numbers of people from countryside to towns, and the introduction of powered machines in most aspects of industry.

INFORMATION TECHNOLOGY Machines, programs, and systems designed to help process information, often more efficiently and reliably than humans can. The best example is computers.

IRRIGATION Systems of dams, canals, pipes, and other tools that help us to maintain a steady water supply to crops, especially in areas with unpredictable rainfall.

Making cathode ray tubes in a factory

LOGARITHM A way to represent numbers as powers of another number, such as 10. The "log" of 100 is 2, because $100 = 10^2$. Logs can represent only positive numbers. Adding logs is equivalent to multiplying the numbers they represent. First slide rules, and then calculators, have made this process automatic.

MECHANICAL Describes actions or events in which the simple laws of motion have a primary role. Often used to describe the activity of machines.

MEDIUM The material or system a signal or energy passes through from one point to another.

MOLECULE The basic unit of a chemical compound, consisting of two or more atoms bonded together. Molecules vary in size. Extremely long molecules are used to make some modern materials, such as Clingfilm.

PHENOMENON An experience or event, particularly as it is sensed by a human observer.

PISTON A flat-headed tubular machine part, which moves up and down within a cylinder. A piston may be mechanically driven to pump gases or fluids in the chamber, or may transfer pressure in the cylinder to drive other parts of the machine.

PIVOT A machine part around which another machine part moves. Pivots may be simple hinges or more complicated structures. They are also known as bearings, since they normally "bear" a load.

PRESSURE The "pressing" force of one substance against another. Usually applies to flexible materials, such as liquids or gases, for example the air inside a car tyre.

PRISM A transparent object, normally glass, used to change the direction of a beam of light. Prisms are often used to split light into separate beams.

RECEIVER The instrument that detects and translates a signal into a form – such as sound waves –- that humans can sense. An everyday example is the radio or "tuner" component in a music system.

RESERVOIR A container for storing liquids, such as machine oil or drinking water.

SEAL A tight join, often using rubber or another waterproof material, which prevents gas or liquid escaping or entering an enclosed space.

SOLUTION In liquids, a solution is a mixture of one liquid with something else – another liquid, a gas, or a solid.

TECHNOLOGY The practical uses of knowledge – in terms of skills, and the creation and use of new tools. New technology is driven both by new scientific discoveries, and new uses for old knowledge.

TRANSMITTER An instrument that translates a signal into a form in which it can be passed through a particular medium to a receiver. Examples include a mobile phone or walkie-talkie.

VACUUM A perfectly empty – or very nearly empty – space. A vacuum can be created in a vessel by pumping out all the gases or liquids inside.

VALVE A flap or plug used to control the flow of gas or liquid from one space to another. Some valves control the direction of flow, some the timing of the flow. Valves are vital for most pumping systems. Their existence in human arteries led scientists to discover the heart's true function – a pump.

Helicopter with its rotary blades in full motion

LEVER A rigid bar, pivoted at one point along its length, used to transmit force. If the distant end of the lever travels further than the load (near the pivot point), the lever "magnifies" the force that can be applied.

LIFT The force required to overcome the weight of a flying machine and keep it off the ground. In an aeroplane, lift is created by passing air over the curved, angled wings. The fast-flowing air pushes against their lower surface and forces the plane up.

Coloured balls represent the arrangement of atoms in a molecule of vitamin B6

This prism is splitting white light into separate beams, revealing a rainbow of colours

Index

Acknowledgments

Dorling Kindersley would like to thank:
The following members of the staff of the Science Museum, London for help with the provision of objects for photography and checking the text: Marcus Austin, Peter Bailes, Brian Bowers, Roger Bridgman, Neil Brown, Jane Bywaters, Sue Cackett, Janet Carding, Ann Carter, Jon Darius, Eryl Davies, Sam Evans, Peter Fitzgerald, Jane Insley, Stephen Johnston, Ghislaine Lawrence, Peter Mann, Mick Marr, Kate Morris, Susan Mossman, Andrew Nahum, Cathy Needham, Francesca Riccini, Derek Robinson, Peter Stephens, Frazer Swift, Peter Tomlinson, John Underwood, Denys Vaughan, Tony Vincent, John Ward, Anthony Wilson, David Woodcock, Michael Wright.
Retouching: Roy Flooks
Index: Jane Parker

Picture credits
t=top, b=bottom, m=middle, l=left, r=right

Ann Ronan Picture Library: 17tl, 29br, 29bm, 35bm, 38tl, 38mr, 44tl, 44tr, 45tl, 56br;
Bridgeman Art Library: 11, 18bm, 19bl; /Russian Museum, Leningrad 21 mr, 22tr; /Giraudon /Musée des Beaux Arts, Vincennes 30bl, 50mr;
British Airways: 68–69m;
Corbis: Haruyoshi Yamaguchi/Sygma 65tr;
Brian Cosgrove Collection: 68-69;
Design Museum: 67bl, 68tl;
E.T. Archive: 26tr;
Vivien Fifield: 32m, 48ml, 48m, 48bl;
Getty Images: Bruce Forster 70bl;
Michael Holford: 16ml, 18,1m, 18bl;
Hulton-Deutsch: 41tr;
Barnabas Kindersley: 64ml;
Mary Evans Picture Library: 10m, 12ml, 12tr, 14, 19mr, 19br, 20tr, 21mr, 23tr, 24tr, 25tr, 28br, 30br, 31mr, 36bl, 39m, 40tl, 40mr, 41tm, 42bl, 42ml, 43tr, 43m, 45tr, 50br, 53mr, 54tl, 54bl, 55ml;
Mentorn Barraclough Carey Productions Ltd: 69br Copyright © 2002 Robot Wars LLC/Robot

Wars Ltd. Trademarks: Robot Wars and the Robot Wars logo are trademarks of Robot Wars LLC. Sir Killalot, Shunt, Matilda, Sgt Bash, Dead Metal, Mr Psycho, Growler and Refbot are trademarks and designs of the BBC in the UK and are used under licence. Sir Killalot, Shunt, Matilda, Sgt Bash, Dead Metal, Mr Psycho, Growler and Refbot are trademarks of Robot Wars LLC in the world excluding the UK. The Robot Wars television series is produced by Mentorn in association with Robot Wars Ltd for BBC Television in the UK and for broadcasters worldwide;
National Maritime Museum, London: 64-65;
National Motor Museum, Beaulieu: 49tr;
Natural History Museum, London: 66tr;
Norfolk Rural Life Museum: 67mr;
Stephen Oliver: 67bl, 68br;
Popperfoto: 64b;
Rex Features: 69tl; /Patrick Barth 65br; /Erik C. Pendzich 65tl;
Science Museum, London: 66br, 70tl, 71b;
Science & Society Picture Library: 63m, 63bl, 63bm, 67ml, 67m;

Syndication International: 12tl, 13m, 23tl, 26mr, 28tl, 28mr, 34tl, 35tl, 36tr, 46br, 50br, 52b, 52tr, 56tr, 58bm, 59br; /Bayerische Staatsbibliotek, Munich 24cl; /City of Bristol Museum and Art Gallery 53br; /British Museum 13tm, 24bl, 59tr; /Library of Congress 37tl; /Smithsonian Institution, Washington DC 58br;
Wallace Collection: 66ml;
Photo Courtesy of Xybernaut Corporation: 64tr

With the exception of the items listed above, and the objects on pages 8-9, 61, and 64-71, all the photographs in this book are of objects in the collections of the Science Museum, London.